Scared SPEECHLESS

Public Speaking
STEP BY STEP

REBECCA McDANIEL

SAGE Publications
International Educational and Professional Publisher
Thousand Oaks   London   New Delhi

For information address:

 SAGE Publications, Inc.
2455 Teller Road
Thousand Oaks, California 91320

SAGE Publications Ltd.
6 Bonhill Street
London EC2A 4PU
United Kingdom

SAGE Publications India Pvt. Ltd.
M-32 Market
Greater Kailash I
New Delhi 110 048 India

Printed in the United States of America

Library of Congress Cataloging-in-Publication Data

McDaniel, Rebecca, 1948–
   Scared speechless : public speaking step by step / Rebecca
McDaniel.
    p. cm.
   Includes bibliographical references and index.
   ISBN-0-8039-5173-6 (cl.) — ISBN 0-8039-5174-4 (pb.)
   1. Public speaking. I. Title.
PN4121.M3397 1994
808.5'1—dc20
                                                      93-29322

94 95 96 97 10 9 8 7 6 5 4 3 2 1

Sage Production Editor: Astrid Virding

Scared
SPEECHLESS

I dedicate this book to my former students,
who have taught me much about teaching;
to my future students,
who will continue guiding me;
and to the memory of Joseph Martin Hansen,
who has directly and indirectly influenced my life
in positive ways.

Contents

Preface

Over the past few years in my beginning speech classes, I have noticed an increase in the number of students who have not had any prior speech course. As I have talked to colleagues from other colleges and universities, I discovered that they, too, have been facing the same type of student. Thus the beginning speech course at the college level is truly "the beginning"—a first-time effort for most students.

As a result of inexperience, students often panic when they enter a speech course and hear the first assignment. When I announce they may choose their own topic for a speech, they ask how they go about choosing one. When I tell them there are time limits, I am asked, "How can we be sure we'll be inside those limits?" When I tell them they need to prepare an outline of their speech, I hear, "What are we supposed to put in an outline?" And on and on it goes with each aspect of preparing a public presentation.

I used to think this hesitation to get started was merely procrastination, but I don't think so anymore. Finally, I realized the problem: Beginning Speech is a singular course often required of non-speech majors; without any training whatsoever, these first-time speech students have no idea of the sequential steps necessary for speech preparation.

To remedy the problem, I have devised (though it has taken 20 years!) a solution: Analyze the exact order of the steps necessary in preparing a speech and teach beginners these steps in sequence. *Scared Speechless: Public Speaking Step by Step* is a speech book that follows this chronological approach, breaking down the steps chapter by chapter in the actual order necessary to arrive at a finished product.

This text is a process book, a how-to text, presented as any set of instructions should be—in logical step-by-step sequence. The logic of chronology is used often in instructions. For example, a computer software package explains steps in sequence from a beginner's perspective; cooking instructions are numbered in the order they are to be completed; hobby projects list steps in a logical order so that the beginner will not have to undo a step because a previous one should have been completed first. When we try to put one of our purchases together with the "do-it-yourself" instructions and have problems, the first target of our anger is usually the confusing instructions that assume we have more knowledge and skill than we actually do. If so many other processes are best understood through simple step-by-step instructions, why not a speech text?

Therefore, this text is not a theory text. Rather it is a hands-on training manual needed by students who are not communication majors and who take speech as a one- or two-quarter course. This text also serves a need by those in the workforce (going back to school) who find themselves expected to deliver presentations but unprepared to do so.

Scared Speechless: Public Speaking Step by Step begins by discussing speech fear. I have discovered speech fear is foremost in the minds of many students, so I deal with it in the first chapter. Depending on the group of learners, some teachers may want to make the first chapter optional. Chapters 2 through 11 name the sequential steps for preparing a public speech. In each chapter, the text presents weak examples of the respective step, discusses why each is weak, and then shows how to make it strong.

The last three chapters (Chapters 12, 13, and 14) are not part of the sequential steps in speech preparation but provide general information on the challenge of persuasive speaking and the process of communication. Chapters 12 and 13 discuss the differences between informing and persuading an audience. Chapter 14 deals with a simplified communication model and describes poor listening habits. Since teachers vary as to when they discuss the communication process and listening skills, Chapter 14 can easily be assigned whenever a teacher deems it most appropriate.

The weakness of all speech texts is that students must be giving speeches as they are learning the steps necessary to do so. Learning any skill has this same inherent problem. The guide at the end of Chapter 1 (and the Appendix) helps the learner realize the series of steps necessary to prepare a speech, and the Appendix also has a well-explained beginning assignment to help students organize when they first begin the formal speaking process.

Special features of this text follow:

1. Has clear, simple, chronological structure.
2. Begins by fully addressing the number one concern of speech students: FEAR.
3. Teaches those skills essential for a beginner to prepare and deliver a speech.
4. Uses only basic terminology.
5. Provides mnemonic devices for easy learning of terms.
6. Gives examples of a wrong way and a right way to accomplish certain skills.
7. Offers detailed samples to illustrate the terms or steps presented.
8. Helps the student get started with in-chapter charts to complete.

Acknowledgments

I am indebted to Sage Publications, Inc., for publishing this text. A special thank you is extended to Sophy Craze, Acquisitions Editor, who worked patiently with me as I struggled in the editing of it. In addition, I would like to thank Ann West, formerly with Sage.

Acknowledgment is made to the reviewers whose comments and constructive criticism has helped me to better the book.

I am grateful to Barney & Barney Graphics for the illustrations. Tad Barney took my ideas and enhanced them beyond words through his creative talents, even though I gave him a very short time span for completion.

I especially thank my colleague and longtime friend Barbara Hansen for reading the rough manuscript and for giving me, as always, encouragement and support for my dreams; and I thank my friend Pamela Miller for reading and rereading the manuscript, making valuable suggestions from a nonteacher's point of view.

1 Taking Advantage of Your Nervousness

I once had a student who approached me after the first day of class and said he was going to withdraw from Speech. He had taken an English class from me the year before, and I remembered him as a good student. In fact, he was almost finished with two years of his degree. He said he just couldn't do it—the "it" meaning speech class. He just could not get in front of a group and talk. I did everything in my power to persuade him to stay. I said I would work with him individually. He said no. I said we could talk to the whole class and get ideas on how to deal with his fear because getting to know the other students and realizing they had sympathy for his plight would help. He still said no. I reminded him that his major area listed speech as a requirement. He said he knew that and, therefore, he was going to change his major. My first reaction was, "You've got to be kidding me." But I could see he was not kidding. That day he changed his major so he would not have to take a speech class.

The sad thing here is that someone changed a major based on the fear of public speaking rather than on the love of a given profession. This fear had literally changed his life.

Sometimes business people who receive a promotion are not prepared when one of the requirements is public speaking. For example, an addictions counselor, promoted to a position requiring him to give occasional speeches, became so anxious that "he passed out in full view of the audience."[1] It is easy to see how speech fear can limit your own job potential, income level, and self-esteem.

What you probably do not realize is that your fear is normal and controllable. In fact, research indicates that many people are scared of public speaking, yet most who fear it never learn there are solutions.

To begin to effectively deal with this fear, it is important that you pinpoint what it is you fear will happen.

Define Your Speaking Fears

When I ask a group, "What is it you fear about speaking in front of a group?" the common response is, "That I will make a fool of myself."

When I ask, "What do you think you would do that would make a fool of yourself," I get various responses: "Forget a word." "Stutter." "Say something stupid." "Shake." "Turn red."

So my next question is, "And what would happen if you did one of these things?"

The typical reply is, "People would laugh at me."

I check their assumption by asking the others what they think they would do if someone in the class were to forget a word or stutter.

The listeners indicate they wouldn't feel like laughing any more than the speaker would. In fact, several claim they would get tense and uneasy because they would feel bad for the speaker.

And when I ask why their responses would be so sympathetic, they say, "Because I know I'll be in the speaker's shoes."

Others Want You to Do Well

The important point is that a beginner of public speaking gains a new attitude because of a new vantage point. You have empathy with another speaker because you know the fear of getting in front of a group. It is the one advantage that being in a group of beginning speakers offers you. All of you have empathy with each other that you might not have otherwise. Hence, everybody will be "pulling" for everybody else to do well. Others want you to succeed. They will be rooting for you to "win" at your performance, just like a sports team cheers each other on to the finish. Always remember: Everybody else is hoping you will succeed. Thus your fear that the audience will laugh at you is really not based on fact. The feelings are self-imposed.

Do Not Expect Too Much From Yourself

Now that we realize the audience reacts sympathetically to us, we can also see more realistically who our critic is: ourselves. We accept errors in others, but we tend to be unaccepting when we ourselves make those same errors. We are frequently harsher judges of ourselves than other people are.

Is it possible to go through a learning experience without making any errors? Could you learn to swim without any problems with form and stroke? Could you learn to play the piano without pushing the wrong keys as you learn? Can you become a golfer by shooting par the first time you take a lesson?

We often expect too much of ourselves. We must accept that we learn a skill partly from the errors we make. We learn any skill by doing it over and over and over—and having a coach help us improve.

That is not to say that you shouldn't work hard to do the best you can. Preparing a speech takes enormous amounts of time and effort to do well, and even professionals look for those areas where they can improve through the use of constructive criticism.

Learn to Accept Constructive Criticism

Personally, I detest being criticized, and I don't know of anyone who doesn't. It is natural for you to dislike the evaluation that will accompany a speech.

I may not like to be criticized, but I know that I have learned a great deal from those who have constructively criticized me. What I have learned from them has helped me achieve success in writing, in speaking, and in professional advancement.

Constructive criticism means that a person is given suggested areas for improvement to become better, to improve. **Destructive criticism** means that the only purpose is to hurt someone through purposeless condemnation. The latter has no positive intentions; the former does.

You must learn to differentiate between these two types of criticism. Your ability to accept constructive criticism is influenced by your past. If you have been constantly criticized, made fun of, or ridiculed, you will have a lower self-esteem than those who have not had this negative environment. You will thus have a more difficult time accepting the advantages of helpful criticism. In case you have not been introduced to the idea that some criticism is positive, I introduce the thought to you now.

Getting suggestions for improvement after a speaking performance does not mean that you have been a failure, that you are dumb, or that you are worthless. Would you expect a basketball or football team, during a time-out, not to be told what they were doing wrong and what to do to correct it? Wouldn't a golfer who hired a pro to teach him or her the game expect to be told if the club was being held wrong or if the swing had major problems? Wouldn't a music instructor inform a student of errors made and how to best correct them? Constructive criticism is the way to improvement. Without it, bad habits develop that not only harm the current performance but also become more and more difficult to break in later performances.

It might help you to avoid the word *criticism* and use *suggestions* instead. The latter is nearer what constructive criticism should do anyway: suggest ways to get better. All trainers and coaches offer suggestions for improvement to those they train, and you are in training. As with most skills, the training itself requires lots of self-discipline, but the nerve-racking aspect is most prominent during the actual performance in front of an audience. Understanding this fear will help a speaker control nervousness.

Understand the Physiology of Fear

Studies of animals' reactions to fear indicate that the onset of fear produces biological changes in the body. In fact, the body's response to a perceived danger is an inborn survival technique that creates the "fight-or-flight" syndrome. For instance, in ancient times in an uncivilized setting when a person was confronted by sudden danger, the body's immediate response to fear was to release adrenaline into the bloodstream. This natural hormone created energy beyond that which was normal in a time of dire need. As a result, if the person decided to opt for the "stay and fight" response, he or she had greater energy than normal to overcome the enemy and survive. If the choice was the "flight" response, the person could run faster than would normally be possible and might be able to escape an enemy that under normal circumstances couldn't be outrun. With either the fight-or-flight option, a physical response occurred that allowed for the **extra** energy to be available for use. If, however, the sudden rush of adrenaline was great enough, the individual could become paralyzed into inaction, unable to move in either fight or flight.

Perhaps you have heard of miraculous stories where a parent who had a child trapped under a car singlehandedly lifted the car and pulled the child to safety. Some of these stories are not the fictional stories from *The National Enquirer* but are from reputable journalists who recorded what happened when fear pumped adrenaline into the body. Adrenaline produces extra **physical** energy.

For example, Marie (Bootsie) Payton from High Island, Texas, discovered that the extra energy produced by adrenaline can save the life of a loved one. Many years ago, Bootsie was mowing the lawn with a riding lawn mower when it got stuck in a ditch. She got off and got it unstuck, and then it got away from her and began going in circles. Unfortunately, her little granddaughter Evie ran in front of the mower, thinking she could stop it—just as she had seen Wonder Woman perform amazing feats on TV. The mower knocked Evie over and began to run over her. Bootsie ran to the mower, grabbed it, and flipped it off her granddaughter. She says that later she tried to lift the mower and couldn't budge it. Though Evie lost four toes, her life was saved because her grandmother took advantage of the adrenaline her body had produced from her sudden fright and managed to do something she couldn't have done under normal circumstances.[2]

The fight-or-flight syndrome still exists; human reaction to fear is biologically the same as in the past. When our mind informs our body that we are nervous, our body reacts by producing adrenaline. Hence, speakers have extra physical energy when they get up in front of an audience. However, they cannot choose between fighting or fleeing (although many would like to run) because these are not options in this civilized setting. The resultant problem is that the extra adrenaline has produced extra physical energy which needs to be released somehow, and it will manage to manifest itself in some **physical** way, positive or negative.

What is important for you to know is that in a public speaking situation, a certain amount of extra energy is desirable; it can improve performance. Also important to know is that too much can produce problems. Our goal is to get rid of the "too much" and keep just enough nervousness to enhance our speech.

We are going to learn how to do just that. At any rate, if you think you want to get rid of your nervousness, think again. Nervousness is desirable and can be a priceless asset for a speaker.

Accomplished Performers Admit Being Nervous

It is normal to fear a public speaking situation, not only for beginning speakers but also for advanced speakers.

In a famous survey mentioned in the *The Book of Answers*,[3] three thousand Americans were asked to rank their fears. The fear of public speaking was ranked number one. Interestingly, death was on the list of choices. Perhaps we can assume people would rather die than give a speech. The late Norman Cousins, world-renowned author and speaker, says that some medical studies indicate that "public speaking is one of the most stressful experiences in any catalogue of human activity."[4]

At least you can realize your fear is normal. You fall into the norm in that most of society gets nervous before a public speech or, for that matter, before any important event. For example, in sports tournaments, in Olympic performances, in the World Series, in a musical debut, don't you think these accomplished performers are "uptight"? Think about the first few shots of a basketball tournament. The excellent shooters miss shots at first, and what do we say? They've got to "loosen up"; they're too "tense." In other words, they've got to get rid of the excess nervous energy typical in an important performance and then turn the remaining extra energy into positive results. It is also in the Olympics that many world records are broken. The excess nervous energy helps produce the best performance of an athlete's lifetime.

On a 1990 segment of the television program *20/20*, John Stossel (ABC news reporter) says he is nervous before each broadcast and paces the floor until just before air time. When he asked Hugh Downs whether he had ever been nervous before a broadcast, Hugh admitted to suffering from mike fright so badly when he was on radio that he had trouble holding his reading material still. This *20/20* segment also pointed out that many famous performers have suffered from performance anxiety. For example, Lawrence Olivier, one of the most acclaimed actors of all time, suffered from extreme stage fright. He called it the "dreaded terror." Likewise, singer Barbra Streisand suffers performance anxiety enough to limit her live performances to one in the past many years.[5] Surprisingly, comedienne Joan Rivers, who performs regularly before live audiences, confesses she always gets stage fright.

It should now be clear to you that fear of performing in front of people is not only a trait of the novice but also of the expert. You are normal when you fear public speaking. More importantly, it is desirable to have some nervousness to heighten the energy of the performance. Stop thinking of nervousness as negative, and realize it is important that you have it! If you are nervous, realize that you are already doing something right in your efforts to learn public speaking.

Notice the Traits Good Speakers Have

I have mentioned the negatives that people fear about public speaking. But now I want to emphasize the positives that help classify speakers as good. The following is a list of positive speaker traits:

Good posture	Interest in subject
Strong eye contact	Caring attitude
Self-confidence	Sense of humor
Enthusiasm	Appropriate gestures
Vocal variety	Interest in audience

At the beginning of this chapter, we looked at the negative feelings people tend to associate with public speaking. These people have a negative mind-set. They are thinking of the bad that might happen during their performance. Note that these negatives are just "possibilities," not realities. There's a famous saying relating to worry: "I am an old man and have had many troubles, most of which have never happened." Much of what we worry about in public speaking will never happen.

Rather than assuming that negatives are the only possibility, we should realize positives are also possible. Some of those positives are named in the above list of good speaker traits. Hence, as with all of life, positives as well as negatives exist. You are the one who decides which you will dwell on, but remember that thinking positively helps you achieve the positive. The following are some ways to help you learn to be a positive thinker about public speaking and begin to instill some of the desirable traits into your own speaking patterns.

Use Positive Imaging Techniques

Try to concentrate on the positive: Picture yourself successfully delivering a dynamic presentation. Emphasizing the positive doesn't mean that the fears will disappear. You feel them, and it is important that you are aware of them. However, begin consciously thinking about the positive speaking traits you would like to have. Begin trying to picture how a speaker who has them uses them, and when you practice, try to instill them in your own performance.

Learn to think positively, similar to the positive imaging that some figure skaters do. They close their eyes and picture every move, every spiral, and every jump that is in their program as it would be if done perfectly. That helps them to then go out and do that performance the way they have pictured it. Positive mental thoughts help you achieve positive physical performances.

Become conscious of any speakers you hear, and note what it is you like about them. Picture yourself giving the same type of positive performance.

Use Relaxation Techniques

Whenever anyone gets nervous, several physical occurrences become evident: The mouth becomes dry; the face or neck flushes; underarms and palms perspire; the stomach feels upset; the bladder fills; the heart races; and breathing becomes faster and shorter than normal. If mental thoughts can affect us physically in a negative way, can't thoughts also produce the opposite effect?

Since nervousness is a mental state, we need to learn to mentally reduce our nervousness. The possibility for doing this exists for all of us; we merely need to learn how and then practice until we see results.

Dr. Herbert Benson popularized the idea that our minds can have some control of our bodies in his book *The Relaxation Response.*

> We will show how high blood pressure is related to stress through the inappropriate elicitation of the fight-or-flight response. Our main purpose, however, is to discuss the Relaxation Response, for it may have a profound influence on your ability to deal with difficult situations and on the prevention and treatment of high blood pressure and its related, widespread diseases including heart attacks and strokes.[6]

Remember that the extra adrenaline pumped by the body results from our mind's fear. Logically, then, if we know what to do to release the fear in the mind, we also will reduce the flow of adrenaline.

The first and most basic concept of gaining control of nervousness involves relaxation breathing. If you were ever in a situation where fear gripped you, you are aware that your breathing suddenly became shallow and frequent. Shallow, quick breaths create more nervousness and, hence, cause you to lose your ability to control either your mind or your body.

Debbie Gardner was just finishing training in Cincinnati to become a police officer and was also nearing completion for her black belt in karate. One evening when she left a party, she was assaulted by a man and froze, unable to protect herself. Fortunately for her, two narcotics agents had left the party immediately after she had and saved her from the attack. Later, in retrospect, she spent months thinking about the incident, wondering why she was unable to respond as she had been trained. Finally, she realized that her inability to react resulted from her faulty breathing; in fact, she said she was paralyzed into inaction because she was actually holding her breath. Her realization that the knowledge of proper breathing was basic to being in control caused her to start her own business (Survive Institute) in self-defense. Her two books, *Survive: Don't Be a Victim* and *Breathe and Believe,* help others learn how to defend themselves. In her seminars and appearances on major network talk shows, her main point is that a person must learn to control breathing in order to be in control of the body.[7]

Lots of research proves that deep breathing creates a relaxation response in the body. Relaxation means to become less tense; if some relaxation comes in, some nervousness goes out. That's a speaker's goal: to gain control by releasing some of the tension. The breathing for relaxation differs from normal breathing; otherwise, we would all be in a constant state of relaxation. I recommend you do the following relaxation exercise alone at home in the privacy of your room as a test for how your body feels after learning to properly perform deep breathing. Then you can modify it for your nervousness before your speech.

1. Sit in a chair with a straight back; do not lie down.
2. Place both feet on the floor; do not cross your legs or sit on one leg.
3. Place your hands on your lap with palms comfortably upward; do not clasp hands.
4. Close your eyes, and try to clear your mind of any thoughts by repeating, "I am getting relaxed."
5. As you slowly inhale through your nose, say "10" and be sure that your stomach area begins to rise. This shows that, rather than inefficient shallow breaths, you are inhaling deep into your lungs, which is extremely important. Inhale until you cannot breathe in another fraction of air.
6. Now exhale slowly through your mouth. If your thoughts start to wander, that's usual. But draw them back to your relaxation sentence you are repeating.
7. Each time you inhale, you will be counting down from ten until you have performed this deep breathing sequence ten times.

Afterwards, pay attention to your body. You have programmed it into a beginning state of relaxation. Some experts are so efficient at relaxation that they can literally change their heart rate, their skin temperature, and also increase their tolerance to pain, as indicated in the following:

> A thermometer was taped to the middle finger of my right hand; it showed that my skin temperature was 76 degrees. I was told that it was within my power, as an act of visualization coupled with will, to increase the temperature of my hands. . . . The person in charge of the exercise spoke to us slowly, putting us in a relaxed state. . . . We were asked to open our eyes and look at the temperature readings. Mine was at 93 degrees. . . . Just to see that I had the ability to affect bodily processes that were supposedly beyond my control was a mind-stretching experience.
>
> Seven biofeedback trainees whom I met at the Menninger Foundation had been migraine patients; all reported unmistakable relief.[8]

In a similar Harvard Medical School study, patients with the circulatory disease called Raynaud's found relief through biofeedback training that "enables them to bring the temperature of their fingers under voluntary control."[9]

Depending on how much you practice this, you can learn to relax briefly just by deep breathing, no matter where you are.

Before you give your speech, you can sit and deep breathe several times to help control your nervousness and, therefore, the adrenaline your body produces. I have gone into detail with the seven steps of relaxation because by doing them, you will be able to feel the relaxation occurring in your body. You need to practice the technique in order for you to realize it is not just a silly exercise but rather a beneficial tool for controlling stage fright.

Do Isometric or Isotonic Exercises

Some people with headaches call their pain a "tension" headache. Frequently, mental tension causes the body to tense. The neck area is a vulnerable place, and stiffening the neck muscles for any length of time often produces stiff necks, sore shoulders, and headaches.

There is no doubt that physical exercising helps reduce tension. The fight-or-flight response means that extra energy is provided in order for the body to physically fight a ferocious battle or perform a record-winning race. Adrenaline's extra provision of energy gets used up, gets physically released, and then the calm returns after the release of the energy.

Admittedly, it would be helpful if you could get up before your speech and do a series of jumping jacks and push-ups to rid yourself of this excess nervous energy, but obviously such blatant exercises aren't feasible. Conspicuous physical exertion may be impossible, but inconspicuous exercise isn't!

Isometric and isotonic exercises work from the same premise. Both work against resistance without obvious physical movement; the only difference is that isometric exercises result in great increase in muscle tone, and isotonic do not. For our purposes, we are merely concerned with the inconspicuous release of physical energy through resisting a stationary source. The resistance is produced by a person's own body or by a stationary object nearby. These exercises still take **energy** to perform, which is the key to their helping reduce nervousness. Below are a few isotonic exercises. **DO EACH ONE SEVERAL TIMES.**

1. Clasp your hands together interlocking your fingers. Push each hand against the other, and then try to pull each hand apart.
2. Sit in a chair and place both feet on the floor. Now attempt to push your feet through the floor's surface and then release the tension.
3. As you sit in a hard chair, drop each hand and grasp the chair seat. Pull up and release; push down and release.
4. If you sit at a desk, place both hands with palms upward under the desk. Push up on the underside of the desk and release. Now place your hands on the top of the desk, push down, and then release.
5. Clench your fists and tighten them as tight as you can and then release them.

Those of you who have training in relaxation know that a part of the technique is tensing different parts of your body and then releasing the muscles. You also know how effective this method is for relieving tension and producing relaxation. The above isotonics should have the same tension-reducing effect, as long as several repetitions are performed.

Practice Your Speech

Usually, after a speaker says the first several words of a speech, nervousness begins to dissipate—if the speaker has rehearsed enough. "Enough" means practicing until the speaker is comfortable with the wording, the note cards, and the delivery. "Enough" means that when the speaker begins the actual presentation in front of an audience, he or she realizes the speech is going to progress just as it has in rehearsals. Such confidence comes only from practicing numerous times.

All the positive imaging, relaxation techniques, and isotonic exercises in the world will not be enough to overcome nervousness if the speaker has neglected to practice. If rehearsals have been short-changed, the delivery will be agonizing, and tension will increase with every word. The reason is because errors will be frequent and pauses will be painfully long. It will be apparent to both speaker and audience that practicing was not a high priority. When the delivery suffers, so does the content. A smooth delivery increases audience understanding; a rough delivery increases audience confusion.

Nervousness will go unnoticed by the audience and will be lessened after the speech begins **only** if the speaker has practiced. Adequate rehearsal is the best guarantee against a negative speaking experience.

Emphasize Speech Content

A sure way for a speaker to help control fear of the audience is to remember the purpose of being in front of the group: to communicate a message. The emphasis is on the word *message*, not yourself. For example, if you can pick a topic that you care about and are involved in, then the desire to share those concerns and that involvement will be a higher priority than the concern of how you look. When you place thinking about yourself as secondary and communicating the message as primary, you will have learned to control nervousness. This is the magic key that opens the door to enjoyable and exciting public speaking. Roger Ailes, media consultant and strategist for many politicians, verifies this idea when he says, "You can learn to control the

atmosphere if you really believe in yourself and understand what
your mission is in every situation."[10] Until you are willing to get involved in your subject matter, you will not speak to your full potential.

To help you recall the above aids to control your nervousness, look
at the first letter of each major word; putting them together spells
PREP (positive imaging, relaxing, exercising, and practicing—with
emphasis on content). You want to PREP yourself as you learn the first
facet of speaking: using nervousness to an advantage. The above techniques are to reduce, not eliminate speech fear; remember, a speaker
needs some nervousness in order to perform energetically.

Anyone Can Become a Good Speaker

You do not have to be formally educated to become a good speaker.
I have listened to speakers holding more than one Ph.D. degree who
gave unbelievably boring speeches. Also, it is a myth that good speakers are born that way. The potential to be a good speaker is already
inside you. The question is, Do you want to tap into it and use it? And
do you have the time for the necessary preparation?

What if I took a magic marker and marked every key on a piano
keyboard and then labeled every note on a score sheet? Would you be
able to sit down and then play the musical piece before you? Of course
not. You would pick and pause and look and hunt and take a long
time to get through just a few of the notes, let alone the whole song.

Similarly, what if I told you the four basic swim strokes and indicated we would have a quiz on the material. I would explain each in
detail, show you slides and drawings, and then give you a quiz. And
let's assume you get a perfect score on the quiz. Does that mean you
know how to swim? Obviously not. In fact, I could take you to a
swimming pool after you had passed the quiz and push you in, and
if you had never swum before, you could drown—**EVEN THOUGH
YOU PASSED A QUIZ ON THE SUBJECT.**

Speaking Is a Skill, Not Just a Body of Knowledge

These examples of learning to play the piano and learning to swim
are similar to learning to speak. Yet the beginning speaker usually is

not aware that speaking follows the same obvious pattern. Speaking is also a skill, and no matter how much of the technicalities you learn, you will not improve until you actually perform. You will improve at a level that directly correlates with the amount you practice. The more you speak in front of an audience, the better you will become. It is just like any other skill. You need knowledge of the subject plus practice using that knowledge.

This book will present the basic sequential steps of speech-making. If you follow the steps, you will know how to prepare an excellent speech, and if you practice, you will become an excellent speaker.

The most important aspect of speaking has to do with the organization of your time in preparing a speech. The following is a sample schedule that can be transferred to a calendar during any month, and it assumes that you have seven days before your speaking engagement. We have not yet covered these steps, but you need to see where you are going as you are learning the steps to get there. All these steps (plus some additional information) are covered in the remainder of this book.

Though you may have only a week to prepare your speech, professional speakers spend more time than you will on preparation; in fact, they often spend two or three months creating a speech, and afterward, they continue to add and delete material to continue improving it.

SPEECH SCHEDULE
BASED ON SEVEN DAYS

Day 1. Choose topic and write personal knowledge about it. Then go to library and check possible subtopics as listed in an index to magazines or on-screen in a computerized library search.

Day 2. Find and read several articles on your topic.

Day 3. Create organization for body of speech and place supporting details from articles and personal experience under the appropriate subdivisions.

Day 4. Write introduction and conclusion.

Day 5. Read speech aloud several times, always timing it, and revising to be within specified time limits; smooth the wording and insert necessary transitions.

Day 6. Place outline on note cards or paper (depending on instructions), rehearsing from the outline, and timing it, continually revising as needed.

Day 7. Rehearse and time speech several times.

Now let's go over the remaining preparation for public speaking step by step. Once you learn to follow these steps, you will never have to worry that you will be scared speechless.

Notes

1. David Sharp, "Send in the Crowds," *Health*, April 1992, p. 68.

2. Story told by Bootsie Payton, High Island, Texas, and used with permission.

3. Barbara Berliner (with Melinda Corey and George Ochoa), *The Book of Answers*, Simon & Schuster, New York, 1992, p. 15.

4. Norman Cousins, *Head First: The Biology of Hope*, E. P. Dutton, New York, 1989, p. 128.

5. Barbara Walters, Hugh Downs, and John Stossel (produced by Karen C. Saunders), *20/20*, ABC Broadcasting Network, June 1, 1990.

6. Herbert Benson, M.D., *The Relaxation Response*, Avon Books, New York, 1976, p. 26.

7. Debbie Gardner, Survive Institute, 7265 Kenwood Road, Cincinnati, Ohio 45236. For a copy of *Breathe and Believe*, write to this address.

8. Norman Cousins, *The Healing Heart*, Avon Books, New York, 1983, pp. 158-159.

9. "Raynaud's Phenomenon," *Harvard Health Letter*, January 1992, p. 3.

10. Roger Ailes, with Jon Kraushar, "How to Make an Audience Love You," *Working Woman*, November 1990, p. 119.

2 Analyzing Your Purpose and Audience

I once listened to a beginning speaker inform an audience about how to shoot a free throw from the foul line in the sport of basketball. After the speech, I asked the audience how many played basketball either currently or in the past. Six responded. I asked those six how many of them knew how to shoot a free throw. Again six responded; they already had the information. I then asked the remaining listeners how many would use the information that had been provided. None responded. I asked how many were interested in the topic as presented, even if they wouldn't use it. Again no one responded. I asked the speaker if he liked basketball. He said he "loved" it. What is the problem in this example? An assumption by a speaker that an audience will be interested in the same subject in exactly the same way as the speaker.

How do we solve the problem? By carefully selecting a speech purpose and then making a topic relate to the audience. Before you can begin to choose a topic or develop it, you must decide a general speech purpose and then learn some facts about your audience.

Decide the General Purpose of Your Speech

First of all, ask whoever invited you to speak what kind of speech the audience wants to hear. There are basically three major speech purposes possible:

1. Persuasive (in which you want your audience to agree with you)
2. Informative (in which you give information, instruction, description, explanation, or demonstration)
3. Entertaining (in which you have key ideas supported by anecdotes, stories, and jokes)

An easy way for you to remember these major speech purposes is to take the first letter of each type of speech, which spells the acronym "PIE."

Persuasive Speaking Is Very Demanding

A persuasive speech ultimately takes one side of a controversial issue, and if you have not had a lot of practice giving speeches, it is not a good idea to start with this type of speech. The persuasive speech has a high level of difficulty and relies on your knowledge of the other types to fulfill its ultimate purpose: to persuade others. This speech purpose is covered in more detail in Chapter 13.

Informative Speaking Is the Most Widely Used and the Simplest

An informative speech is the most common speech type or purpose. It is used constantly throughout life, as we are continually seeking and distributing information. The difficulty in this type of speech is that a speaker must work hard to make something easy to understand and must also be creative enough to make the information interesting rather than boring. The informative speech does not take sides; rather it passes along information—even if the topic is of a potentially controversial nature. With such a topic, the informative speaker is obligated to give a balanced view of *both* sides of the issue. Other important points for an informative speaker is that the information be NEW to the audience, not something many already know, and that it not be too technical for the audience to understand. Though the topic itself may be familiar to the audience, the speaker needs to find a novel approach that will create relevance and maintain interest.

An Entertaining Speech Is the Most Enjoyable for the Audience, But Not the Easiest for the Speaker

An entertainment speech (sometimes referred to as a speech to evoke) is usually used for after-dinner occasions when a festive, light-hearted atmosphere exists. Many people mistakenly think this kind of speech is just a series of jokes (as some stand-up comic routines are). On the contrary, an entertainment speech is actually a formal speech organized around main ideas. The difference from the other speech types is in the tone and the support. Usually the details consist of amusing anecdotes and stories, with an occasional joke. The difficulty with this type of speech is that different people have different senses of humor. What you think is funny, someone else may find humorless. Norman Cousins notes this when he says, "One man's humor is another man's ho-hum."[1]

Beginners Should Master the Informative Speech First

Realizing that a beginning speaker will experience success more easily by creating and delivering an informative speech, that type is the one we will concentrate on. We inform others constantly. We give someone directions on the simplest route to get somewhere. We explain an assignment. We tell a friend the problems we've had with our car. We describe an article of clothing we wanted but couldn't afford. We explain to the repair person what is wrong with the appliance. At work our boss asks that we explain the job responsibilities to the newly hired employee. And the list of our daily informative speaking goes on and on.

For a public speaker who is selecting a topic to inform an audience, the most important question to ask is, What information can I give my audience that is new, interesting, and useful to *them?* Even if the topic is a common one, the speaker needs to analyze the audience in order to know the best approach to take.

For example, if a speaker chooses to discuss car mechanics and discovers the audience has no interest in working on their own cars, that speaker must figure a way to relate the topic to the level of knowledge and interest of the audience. The speaker needs to approach the topic **from the listeners' perspective.** So the speaker must begin thinking about possible angles of the topic. Often this is accomplished by asking questions about the topic using the **what, why, when, where,** and **how** method reporters use.

If we still want to talk about cars to this audience that has little interest in working on their own vehicles, we need to find a way to talk about cars that would interest them. By using some of the reporters' question-words, we might arrive at the following:

WHAT?

- What about cars would interest listeners who do not work on their own cars?
- What are they directly involved with in terms of their own cars?

WHY?

- Why should anyone bother having basic car maintenance done?
- Why should a buyer do research before bargaining for a new car?

WHEN?

- When can a car buyer invoke the "Lemon Law"?
- When should you say no to "the best deal in town?"

WHERE?

- Where do the first problems with a car most often appear?
- Where are the best or quickest fast oil-change service centers?

HOW?

- How does a buyer of a new or used car learn to effectively bargain?
- How does a person keep from being overcharged for a repair?

You should get the idea here that the speaker is thinking about the listeners. A topic is chosen using two criteria: (1) speaker interest and (2) audience interest.

This audience analysis is necessary whether you have been hired to speak to a group of strangers or asked to donate a speech to a group of friends. Here are some of the questions you should ask about any audience.

Ask Questions About Your Audience

You should keep in mind that if a speaker already has a topic in mind, these questions vary in relevance. That is, some become important, and many may become unnecessary.

1. Gender (What is the ratio of males to females?)
2. Age range (What are the youngest and oldest age? In what range does most of the audience fall?)
3. Spare-time activities (Are audience members diverse in interests?)
4. Socioeconomic status (What area of society do members of the audience belong to? What is their income level?)
5. Race (What races and ethnic groups are represented in the audience membership?)
6. Religion (Does the audience represent a wide variety?)
7. Education (What are the lowest and highest degrees? What education does most of the audience have?)
8. Occupation (What are the part-time or full-time jobs, and what are the job goals for the future?)
9. Occasion (What is the reason for everyone gathering to hear you speak? Are they present to celebrate, to learn, or to debate? A special occasion will frequently narrow a topic choice.)
10. Relationship (How are the listeners related? What do they have in common? Are all or many in the same occupation, club, neighborhood?)

In most cases, answers can be gotten from the individual who asks you to speak; after all, if you have been asked to speak to a group, the members have something in common—or they wouldn't be gathering as a group. If you have not been told in advance, your job is to ask what topics most interest the members.

Some speakers use a charting method, creating a list of audience demographics and an easy way to quickly visualize the makeup of the audience. This type of analysis becomes important when the group is diverse. A couple of instances when this diversity might occur are in a class or in a general seminar. The chart contains categories divided into two columns, one for females and one for males. If you distribute this to an audience, you tell the females to place check marks under the female column and the males under the male column. Thus when you do the final tabulation, you know the female/male ratio for every demographic characteristic.

Let's look at why gender is important. Recently a friend of mine attended a workshop consisting of all nurses. The audience consisted of nineteen females and one male. One of the speakers, a male hazards communication director, consistently referred to how "man" is affected by certain chemicals and what "he" should do about it. The constant usage of male nouns and pronouns became offensive to many of the listeners. Had the speaker been conscious of the importance of gender, he would have changed his wording to include both females and males.

Today's society has less of the old social separation between men's and women's roles. America's population has both female and male nurses, doctors, carpenters, engineers, plumbers, housekeepers, and construction workers. Though there is less of the traditional role-distinctions of our past, women are still socialized differently from men. The speaker's task is to analyze the listeners in order to know the best way to approach a topic.

Guidelines on non-offensive gender language suggest that wherever possible, a speaker use nonsexist language. For example, the use of the plural pronouns wherever possible eliminates sexual distinction. The hazards communication director could have achieved nonsexist language by saying "people" (rather than "man") are affected by chemicals and "they" (rather than "he") should know what to do in case of exposure.

Table 2.1 shows a sample chart of possible categories by which you can classify an audience. It is often impossible to get all this information about the audience, and frequently, depending on the speech topic, some information is unneeded anyway. For example, if you decided to speak about investments, you would definitely need to know the listeners' education level, socioeconomic status, ages, occupations, and whether they have dependents. However, you would likely not need to know their religious background.

The answers to the most important questions reveal how you should handle the topic. For example, you could use business and investment terminology if your audience were middle-aged, college educated, top management professionals. However, you would deal differently with the topic if your audience were a group of new graduates.

You can see that if you already know a topic you want to speak on, you will know which questions about the audience are important; the answers show you **how** to deal with the topic for that particular audience. If the speaker who demonstrated a free throw had asked his audience in advance about their basketball knowledge and then had asked questions about what **the listeners** might find interesting about basketball, he might have been able to use the topic of basketball but with a different approach. For instance, he might have told the audience about one of the few sports that is totally American—created here in a very different way than we now know it. Then he could have discussed its history, how it used to be played, and how today's sport differs drastically from the past. Without asking and answering the questions relevant to your particular topic, however, you may find yourself in an uncomfortable situation.

But what if you do not have a topic already in mind? Then answering a variety of questions about the audience may help you decide on an appropriate topic.

Let's hypothetically analyze two audiences. The first, after analysis, consists of all females, married, in an age-range from 19 to 55, all with children, and all holding jobs as either receptionists, secretaries, or office managers. The second group has all the characteristics above, except they are all divorced.

You could speak to either group about the major problems of raising a child in today's society or about how to climb the promotional ladder into a management position. But the topics of how to raise a child

Table 2.1 Possible Audience Classification Categories

	# Females:	# Males:
Age Range:		
Preteens		
Teens		
Twenties		
Thirties		
Forties		
Fifties		
Sixties +		
Spare-Time Activities:		
Sports		
Family		
Computer		
Sciences		
Reading		
Writing		
Volunteer Work		
Crafts		
Other:_____		
Socioeconomics:		
Lower		
Lower Middle		
Middle		
Upper Middle		
Upper		
Race:		
Afro-American		
Asian American		
European American		
Native American		
Hispanic American		
Other:_____		
Religion:		
Protestant		
Catholic		
Jewish		
Atheist		
Agnostic		
Other:_____		
Education:		
No Degree		
G.E.D.		
H.S. Diploma		
College Diploma		
Post Graduate		
Occupations: (fill in)		
_____		
_____		
_____		
_____		
Occasion:		

alone, how to raise a child without a male role model, how to avoid the negatives of single-parent families, or how society labels and limits the divorced parent would be appropriate only to the second group, not the first.

The more information a speaker can discover about the audience, the easier it is to choose a topic.

Ask Questions About Your Speaking Environment

Not only do you need to analyze your audience, but also you should gain knowledge about the room in which you will be speaking. How big is it? How many chairs does it hold? How many will be in the audience? Is there a chalk board, an overhead projector, a slide projector and screen? If you are going to use posters, is there a place to put them so the whole audience can see? How will you keep the posters upright for the listeners to see? Is the room big enough to need a microphone? If so and if you have never spoken with one before, you better arrive plenty early to do a rehearsal so you do not run into problems.

Furthermore, you need to ask how the listeners will be arranged. Depending on the layout of the chairs or tables, a speaker must decide which visual aids are best. For example, when the seating is arranged so all chairs line up in straight rows, the persons sitting behind anyone else and looking straight ahead will be watching the back of someone else's head. Depending on where the speaker is standing, some listeners' views are likely to be blocked. An arrangement that is considered to be better than straight rows is a curved line for each row so that a kind of semicircle is created. The listeners can more easily see both the speaker and the visual aids. Whether or not you, as a speaker, have control over the seating arrangement of the listeners, you must always watch the audience for their nonverbal signals, checking to see if they are having a hard time seeing you or the visual aid. You may need to move around somewhat, or you may need to reposition your visual aid. Paying attention to your audience and making adjustments for their sake will help them have a positive impression of you.

If your speech purpose is not decided for you when you are asked to speak, then you may want to do an audience analysis before you decide whether to inform, persuade, or entertain. Doing an adequate analysis of your listeners may help you establish which of these three purposes would be the best suited for a given audience. Keep in mind, though, that as a beginner, the informative speech tends to be the simplest. Once you know your speech purpose, you have to choose a topic, decide what information you need about your audience, and devise the best method of getting that vital information. You then tailor your speech based on what you have learned about your audience and your speaking environment.

Note

1. Norman Cousins, *Head First: The Biology of Hope*, E. P. Dutton, New York, 1989, p. 126.

3 Selecting Your Method of Delivery

Now that you have selected your speech purpose and realize the importance of analyzing your audience so that you can achieve your goals, you need to be aware of some choices you have in delivering your speech. Though strategies for effectively presenting your speech are discussed in a later chapter, an awareness of the basic methods of delivery will be helpful as you begin putting a speech together. The decision to place delivery methods before selection of a topic is a result of many beginning speakers wanting to know just how they will be presenting information, whatever the topic may be. In fact, one of the first questions asked by beginning speakers is, Should I write it out and read it or memorize it? That question is answered in this chapter, which explains some of the choices you have when delivering your speech.

There Are Essentially Four Methods of Delivery

Now that you know you must choose one of three speech purposes and should analyze the audience, you need to understand your options in delivering the information. Basically, there are four ways you can present the information you have:

1. Manuscript reading
2. Impromptu
3. Memorized
4. Extemporaneous

Note that the first letter of each of these delivery types creates the word *MIME.* The irony about this acronym is that a mime communicates without using any words; a mime acts out physically what he or she wants communicated.

No matter what your general purpose in speaking (to persuade, to inform, or to entertain), you must also decide the method of delivery that is best for the audience and the occasion.

Manuscript Reading Is Done in Special Circumstances

This first type of delivery is defined by the term *manuscript reading.* The speech is read from a manuscript word for word. This reading of a speech should be done rarely because of inherent problems, but there are times when it is important to use such a delivery. The most obvious person using this method is the President or a spokesperson for him, when the media will sift, sort, and scrutinize every word. In fact, the speech or sections of it will likely be published in the paper. Segments of it will be rerun on radio and television. The same is true of someone making an important announcement to society. For example, an oil company that has accidentally dumped millions of gallons of oil in the ocean will send a spokesperson to appear before the media and read a carefully constructed statement. Ad-libbing in this case can be dangerous to company image. So, at very important times when errors dare not exist, a speaker will speak using a "manuscript reading" delivery. But there are problems inherent in such a delivery, especially for a beginning speaker.

Know the Disadvantages of Reading From Manuscript

1. When a speaker is busy looking down at a manuscript in order to read it, he or she cannot look at the audience. The result is loss of eye contact with the listeners, which makes them feel unimportant and insignificant.
2. Frequently a read speech sounds like it is being read. A reading voice is frequently a monotone, without expression or vocal variety or interest. The audience is quick to become bored and to stop listening.
3. When a speaker spends so much time looking down at the speech, he or she cannot watch for audience feedback and thus loses the chance to react to the audience's needs.

Impromptu Speaking Occurs on the Spur of the Moment

Think of the times you have been in a class or in a meeting and have been asked your opinion about some idea being discussed. There in front of a group of people, you must deliver a short speech. When you are at work and the manager asks you about how you handled a problem, you must give a short spur-of-the-moment speech. When an important event occurs and newscasters suddenly must go on air, they must avoid long silences by ad-libbing. When the President holds a press conference and journalists ask questions, he must give an impromptu response (though he will have rehearsed various possibilities beforehand).

Impromptu means that the speaker has no time to prepare. I recall in my college days a speech teacher who enjoyed impromptu speeches and required each student to bring in an object. We were told we would not get it back and it was, therefore, to have little value. Then at the end of each class when there was time left over after the speeches of the day were finished, he would call on one of us to reach into the box where the objects were stored and pull out one object. Then we were to give a three-minute speech on the object. We could do any type of speech we wanted; we could even make up some ideas for

entertainment, but we never knew in advance when we would be called upon or what object we would draw. Now that's impromptu in the extreme!

This assignment may sound cruel, and I admit it was nerve-racking, but it taught us to have some general ideas ready in advance so that what seemed like an impromptu was not totally on the spur. Advance thinking is the secret of this type of speech. You can predict when you might be asked to say something "off the cuff." For example, if you belong to a club or organization that meets regularly and invites speakers from outside, you know someone has to introduce the guest of the evening. Though there may be a designated member who usually performs this function, he or she is bound to be absent sometime. And then someone else will be asked to do the job. That someone may be you. Similarly, a coincidence may occur when both the president and the vice-president of the club are absent. Another member will be asked to be the temporary fill-in. You should heighten your awareness of such potential situations in your life so that you are ready when (not if) the time comes. In other words, predict possibilities when you might be called on to deliver impromptu, and you will make a good impression. Mark Twain, American author and humorist, claimed that expert speakers know that the "best and most telling speech is not the actual impromptu one, but the counterfeit of it; they know that speech is most worth listening to which has been carefully prepared in private . . . until the speaker . . . will seem impromptu to an audience." [1]

Know the Disadvantages of the Impromptu

1. Having no time to prepare for this speech, the speaker is often disorganized and lacks the needed details to support main ideas, if by some miracle main ideas exist. The content is therefore usually weak.
2. Resulting from lack of preparation, the speaker's delivery is a fumbling one often filled with awkward silences and repeated phrases, such as "you know," "see what I mean," "uh," and other pet phrases.

Memorized Speaking Is Learned Word for Word

There aren't very many speakers who can memorize a speech verbatim and make the performance look natural. This method of delivery is very time consuming and usually is done out of fear of not being able to converse naturally with an audience about main ideas. In other words, it is a maneuver to alleviate the fear of public speaking, but the opposite outcome usually occurs. It is a tactic in which total control is the goal, but ironically the speaker loses the very thing that is sought.

Surely you have memorized something before, and then when you got up to recite, your brain has gone blank. And even if you started all right, you probably got to some word and then couldn't remember what was next. At that point the only way to get through the piece is to start clear back at the beginning and plod through material you have already covered and hope when you get to the troublesome spot, the forgotten word comes back to you. The reason you have to go clear back to the beginning is that if a piece is *totally* memorized, it has been learned word for word. This type of memorization means that every separate word relies on the one before it and after it. Main ideas are not what has been learned but rather verbatim wording, as a person would memorize a poem word for word.

Dale Carnegie, in *The Quick and Easy Way to Effective Speaking,* tells the delightful story of an insurance salesman asked to give a speech in front of an audience of two thousand. The salesman decided to memorize his speech so it would go smoothly. When he got up to deliver it, he went blank. Each time he went blank, he would back up a step and try again. Finally he toppled off the back of the platform he was standing on and disappeared. Members of the audience laughed so hard they fell out of their chairs.[2] Though you can see the humor from the audience's view, you can also feel the humiliation from the speaker's experience. Quite simply, it happened because a nervous speaker thought memorizing would put him in control of the speaking situation; as usually happens with memorization, it left him totally out of control.

Know the Disadvantages of the Memorized Speech

1. The biggest disadvantage of memorizing a speech is that the delivery sounds memorized to the audience; this is often called a *canned delivery.* The term was coined from the television situation comedies when not performed in front of a live audience. The laughter the audience hears is on tape and is turned up and down wherever the editor wants the audience to laugh. Though the laugh track is more sophisticated than when it first came into being, an audience can tell it is artificial. A memorized delivery also sounds artificial.

2. With memorization comes the tendency to speak in a monotone or in a sing-song fashion with the same limited vocal variety over and over.

The wide range of pitch variety is not possible because natural conversation differs from the artificiality of memorization.

3. A speaker who memorizes loses the ability to be spontaneous with the audience. Unlike a manuscript delivery, the memorized delivery does allow the speaker to have eye contact with the audience. But still one of the same problems exists for both the manuscript and the memorized delivery: The one who memorizes doesn't dare react to the audience and ad-lib because then the speaker would forget the rest of the speech.

4. Of course, the most obvious downfall of memorizing a speech is forgetting a word and being unable to continue. The odds of such an occurrence are great enough to make memorizing a speech not worth the risk.

Extemporaneous Speaking Is Both Planned and Spontaneous

The extemporaneous speech is a mixture of the good of the other three types of delivery without the bad. It is planned in advance, as are the manuscript reading and the memorized. But unlike the manuscript reading, only key words, not the whole script, are placed on note cards or in an outline. Thus the speaker does not have to read, but merely looks at the note card or outline and then converses about the idea with the audience. Since the speech is not memorized, there is no worry about forgetting a word and not being able to continue.

However, I have had worried students tell me that they have rehearsed enough times they fear they have memorized parts. The key here is that memorizing little sections is not a memorized speech. If you memorize enough that you cannot go on without going back to the beginning, then you have memorized too much. But if you memorize main ideas and a couple words here and there and do not rely on word-for-word delivery, then there isn't a problem. And do not forget that you have practiced from notes (not a written-out speech) and have redone them during practices so that you have main ideas, key words, and any trouble spots to help you recall the order of your comments. The notes are for you to use so that you can be conversational.

Also, unlike the impromptu, the extemporaneous delivery is one that is planned and practiced in advance so that there are no agonizing silences because of having no organization or details.

Know the Advantages of the Extemporaneous Delivery

1. The extemporaneous delivery is organized in advance and, therefore, presents main ideas for the audience to follow.
2. This method permits reading and researching in advance of the speech, which also allows for adequate supporting details and explanation of ideas.
3. Since an outline can be used, there is no need to memorize the speech, thus minimizing the possibility of not being able to continue because of forgetfulness.
4. Because of rehearsing several times, the speaker can have strong eye contact and also spontaneously react to audience feedback.
5. Because the speech is not memorized or read, the speaker can be conversational and use natural pitch variety and word emphasis.
6. The rehearsals allow the speaker to ensure that he or she is within the specified time limits.

This last point is very important. One of the biggest breaches by speakers is going outside the time limitations given. Though some speakers might consider time limitations to be irrelevant, the negatives that occur indicate otherwise.

Speaking without rehearsing enough that you know you are within the time limits is a self-centered action. Every audience is angered by and resentful of such inconsiderate behavior.

There is a well-known little saying about the three vital keys to good speaking: (1) Be brief, (2) be sincere, and (3) be seated.

Your initial analysis when first planning a speech should take into consideration not only factors about the listeners and a decision on the purpose of the speech but also the type of delivery that is best suited to the audience and purpose. For most beginners, the initial speeches will be informative in purpose and extemporaneous in delivery.

Notes

1. Charles Neider, ed., *The Complete Essays of Mark Twain*, Doubleday & Company, Inc., Garden City, 1963, p. 641 (in an essay titled "On Speech-Making Reform").
2. Dale Carnegie, *The Quick and Easy Way to Effective Speaking*, Dale Carnegie & Associates, Inc., Garden City, 1962, pp. 33-35.

4 Choosing Your Topic

What would make you personally want to listen to an informative speech?

Though there may be a variety of factors, one of the most important and basic is that it is interesting to you. Audiences will listen if they are interested in the subject.

Fulfill Two Prerequisites When You Select Your Topic

You have two prerequisites for picking a good topic for a speech. The first is that you, as a speaker, are interested in the topic. If you are not interested, then you will deliver the speech in an uninteresting, boring way. You must be interested in your topic in order to give yourself an edge as a speaker.

The second prerequisite for selecting a good topic is much harder than the first: You must pick a topic that the **audience** is interested in. You have to figure an angle of this topic you are interested in so that the whole audience finds it interesting also. This means you probably will not be using the topic in exactly the way you now know it.

For example, at the beginning of Chapter 2 you learned about a speaker who chose to inform an audience about how to shoot a free throw.

When this speaker decided to speak on one aspect of playing basketball, he created a problem for himself: Those in the audience who play or watch basketball do not need to learn how; they already know the basics. Those listeners who do not play or watch the sport evidently have never been interested enough to want to find out, or they would be doing it.

So, thinking about how the audience will respond is vital to getting a topic of interest. However, if the speaker can find an angle to the topic of basketball that will be interesting to both those who know and care about the sport as well as those who do not, the topic will be a great idea. On the other hand, if the topic cannot be made interesting to the whole audience, the topic does need to be discarded and a different one chosen.

It's the good speaker who spends the time and effort to discover how to make the topic interesting to the audience. More about this later, but first let's figure how to give ourselves lots of topic choices.

Brainstorm to Get a List You Can Choose From

When I tell my students that they can pick any topic they want, they often respond by saying they do not know any speech topics. If that is the way you feel, let me assure you that you do know some topics. The way to find out what they are is to brainstorm about your past, your present, and your future. You possess knowledge about a variety of topics; the problem is getting a list of your possibilities. The biggest mistake made by beginning speakers is to try to prepare the first or second topic that comes to mind. Giving yourself ample choices increases your chances of finding a topic interesting not only to yourself but also to others.

One way to begin this process is to create a spreadsheet to be filled in by you. The left-hand column lists general categories of life, and the horizontal row at the top of the spreadsheet suggests that (where applicable) you think of your past life, your present existence, and your future plans in terms of each category listed in the left column.

You can use the spreadsheet in Table 4.1 and fill in any areas applicable. For example, in the first one on travel, list places you have been. Do not assume that you must have gone to some exotic foreign country to have anything interesting to say; that is far from true. You may not even have gone out of your own state but yet have found some interesting spots. Put any festivals, special events, historical buildings, or interesting side trips you have taken. Put down as many things as you can think of. And if you have any trips in the planning stages, put that under the "present" column. For the future column, you will put down any places you would like to go if you had the time and the money. By filling in the future slot, you are identifying places that are interesting to you. This creates possible topics to research and find interesting facts about. This brainstorming begins to help you find the areas about which you either already have knowledge (the past column, which you have experienced previously, or the present column, which you are experiencing currently in your life) or areas in which you are interested in getting some knowledge (the future column).

During brainstorming, do not worry about spelling, overlapping topics, or ideas that don't seem to fit quite right. Rather, write whatever comes to mind. You are giving yourself an option list for any number of speeches you may give. The more options you give yourself, the better the opportunity for a good topic. An example of a completed chart is shown in Table 4.2.

Once you fill in as many available slots as possible, you will see that you have quite a bit of experience and knowledge about a wide variety of topics. These topics are potential springboards for your speech material.

By filling in the brainstorming information, you have fulfilled the first prerequisite in selecting a speech topic: providing yourself a topic in which you, the speaker, are interested. You have given yourself an advantage by creating choices: The more choices, the more likely you are to find a good topic. But you still have a disadvantage: You cannot be assured the audience will be interested, which is the second prerequisite of selecting a topic. Very likely, the way you are interested in many of your topics will not be the same way that the audience will be interested.

Table 4.1 Brainstorming Chart

Past	Present	Future
Traveling:		
Unusual Travel Experiences:	Here there is nothing for present or future	
Hobbies:		
Sports (participant or spectator):		
Crafts:		
Special Interests:		
Volunteer Work:		
Jobs:		
Expertise (repairs, creative projects, collections):		
Past Accidents:	XXXX	XXXX
Pets:		
Types of Magazines & Books:		
Music Tastes:		
Personal Problems (diseases, addictions, abuses, handicaps, dysfunctional families):		

Table 4.2 Sample Completed Brainstorming Chart

	Past	Present	Future
Traveling:	Art museum, History museum, Chicago, Los Angeles, N.Y.C., Nat'l Parks, Amish country in Pennsylvania	planned camping trip	Paris, London
Unusual Travel Experiences:	Made friends with Amish family and rode in buggy. Toured Amish family building where buggies are made and sold as business. Experience with bear at Daniel Boone Nat'l Park Robbed on trip to Florida		
Hobbies:	collect keys, collect coins, pen pal	gardening, ham radio, writing, dog-training	parachuting, traveling
Sports (participant or spectator):	football, baseball, basketball	Frisbee-golf, miniature golf, karate, bicycling, camping	guns, golf, racquetball
Crafts:	cross-stitching, carpentry, assembling electronic kits	carpentry,	painting, & drawing
Special Interests:		reading about health and self-help psychology	health, psychology, ham radio, history of feminism
Volunteer Work:	horseback riding for the handicapped, tutoring in English	none	helping people with AIDS, ham radio disaster work
Jobs:	farmwork, KFC employee	tutoring	run own business, write, teach
Expertise (repairs, creative projects, collections):	car maintenance	basic car repair, household repairs, finish unfinished basements	coin collecting, stamp collecting, learn finish-carpentry
Past Accidents:	car wreck, nail in foot, wasp sting		
Pets:	dogs, horses, sheep, calf, cats	2 dogs	more dogs
Types of Magazines & Books:	BOOKS	ham-radio, Ms. Magazine, self-help, feminism, health	wood projects, ham radio, news magazines
Music Tastes:	rock & roll	oldies but goodies, country, jazz, soft instrumental, piano, clarinet, flute	classical
Personal Problems (diseases, addictions, abuses, handicaps, dysfunctional families):	dysfunctional family	friend has rare disease, another friend is paraplegic, various friends have had addictions: eating disorder, alcoholism	

Beware of a Topic
Only a Few Would Find Interesting

Let's return to that basketball topic mentioned earlier. We already established the audience was not interested in learning how to shoot a free throw. Though his own interest in basketball is why the speaker chose this topic, the speaker did not fulfill the second prerequisite when selecting a topic: How is he going to relate this topic to the audience?

The first problem is that if they also enjoy basketball, the speaker is not giving them **NEW** information; they already know the rules. And in an informative speech, if information is not new, why give it? The second problem is that if the other audience members wanted to pursue the sport of basketball, they would have done so by now. They are not interested in knowing about it. Basically, in our society we already know about baseball, basketball, football, golf, and soccer. To give us the rules or instructions in those areas is to give us information we have readily available to us if we care to know. So you have to be careful with the area of sports. If you use it, give new and different information.

Your first impulse may be to say, "Okay, let's throw out that topic idea." But don't be too hasty. There are other angles of the basketball topic that can interest a wide variety of listeners. For example, what about where and how basketball was created? It is one of the few sports actually created in America and has been dubbed America's most important gift to sports.[1] Some of the beginning rules are surprising. How have they changed? When was the first competition? What were uniforms of the past like? When did players first get paid? When were women allowed to play? These are some of the facts about basketball that anyone would find interesting or amusing. It is the speaker's responsibility to find what would be interesting to the audience.

Another possibility with the topic of sports is to discuss an unusual sport, one that is not so common: skydiving, spelunking, darts, judo, and so forth. And then tell the audience the most fascinating aspects of the sport. Always ask yourself, "What would the audience find interesting and new?"

Now look at the following list as additions to the topic selection you have just provided yourself. An advantage of using your own list is that you already have some knowledge about the topic. But if you find that you do not want to use your listing, you can use the ones in the table. Pick your topic based on your interests and your analysis of what the audience would find interesting.

ABUSE OF THE ELDERLY	DIFFERENT CULTURES	LITTERING
ACCIDENTS	DISEASE	LOSING WEIGHT
ACID RAIN	DISORGANIZATION	MANNERS
ADDICTIONS	DOGS	MARTIAL ARTS
ADVERTISING	EATING DISORDERS	MEDICINAL HERBS AND
ALZHEIMER'S DISEASE	ELDERLY	PLANTS
AMATEUR RADIO	EMERGENCIES	MENTAL HEALTH
ASSERTIVENESS	ETIQUETTE	MENTAL ILLNESS
ATTITUDE	EXERCISING	MONEY-MAKING HOBBIES
AUTO REPAIRS	FAST FOODS	MUSIC
BETTING	FEAR	MUSIC THERAPY
BIOFEEDBACK	FIRST AID	NATURAL DISASTERS
BODY-PRODUCED DRUGS	FOOD ABUSE	NEWS REPORTING
BUDGETING	FUNERALS	NUTRITION
BUYING A USED CAR	GENERIC DRUGS	ORGAN DONATION
CAMPING	GENETICS	ORGANIZATION
CANOEING	GRIEVING	PAINTING
CAR MAINTENANCE	HEALTH	PART-TIME JOBS
CHANGING BAD HABITS	HEREDITY	PET OWNERSHIP
CHEMICAL PEELS	HOLIDAY HISTORIES	PET THERAPY
CHILD CUSTODY RIGHTS	HOLISTIC MEDICINE	PHOTOGRAPHY
CHILD SEXUAL ABUSE	HOMEOPATHY	PMS
CHILD REARING	HOME MAINTENANCE	POLLUTION
CITY SITES	HOME REPAIRS	PRESCRIPTION DRUGS
CLAIRVOYANCE	HORSEBACK RIDING	PRIORITIES
COLLECTING	HOSPICE	RADIO
COMMERCIAL ART	HOT AIR BALLOONING	RAPPELLING
COMPUTER THERAPY	HYPNOTISM	REFINISHING
COOKING	ILLNESS	ROLE MODELS
COPING WITH BAD HABITS	INEXPENSIVE VACATIONS	ROLE REVERSAL
COSMETICS	KAYAKING	SAFETY
CRIMES	LASERS	SALARIES
CUTLERY	LAWS	SELF-DEFENSE
CYCLING	LEARNING DISABILITIES	SELF-ESTEEM
DEATH	LITERACY	SEX EDUCATION
DIETS		

You might want to pick two topics you like. There are a couple of reasons for this. One is that you may discover that after working on a topic for a while, you do not like the topic or it is too difficult or information is not readily available. At any rate, let's assume the topic is not working the way you thought it would. By choosing two potential topics, you can go to your second choice and work on that one without wasting time going back through the original listing again.

You Must Relate to Your Audience's Interests and Needs

The second reason for picking two topics has to do with your audience. After you have picked two topics, you should go back and rate them according to preference: 1st choice and 2nd choice. After you number them, again go back, but now number them from a different perspective. Which topic do you think your **audience** will be most interested in? Number them according to what you think the audience's preference would be. If the numbering for the audience differs from the numbering for your personal preference, you might want to choose the topic that the audience is most interested in. First of all, it is one of your top two choices, so you are interested in it. Secondly, it will likely be easier for you to create the speech with your audience in mind, since you have already indicated that you think the audience has some interest. Your reason for speaking is to get your knowledge and ideas to your listeners. Those listeners must be interested or they will stop listening.

I should point out that when you are not in a course on effective speaking, you will not likely be so fortunate as to choose any topic you wish. That is, you will probably be expected to give business presentations, instructions, or information sessions. If you are asked to deliver a presentation to a specific group, you may be told a topic to discuss or be given a narrow range of topics. Yet, you still must analyze your audience and relate to their interests and needs. The person who remembers this advice will make a positive impression—one superior to those who neglect this important facet of speaking.

Beware of Sexual Stereotyping in Your Topic

We are a society struggling with sex roles. There are still more male mechanics than female mechanics, more housewives than househusbands, more female secretaries than male. Hence, there can still be a tendency to speak from a biased sex-role perspective. Yet social roles are changing—even if slowly. We do have female firefighters and male nurses, female construction workers and male receptionists, female politicians and male secretaries.

So should a speaker orient a speech according to traditional roles or new roles? The answer is that speakers should analyze the audience in order to present an appropriate topic in a non-offensive way.

For example, if after evaluating the audience, a female who desires to discuss cross-stitching discovers that the audience is basically traditional, she will know that most of the males will not be interested. In fact, they may even be uncomfortable with the idea of their doing any cross-stitching. Indeed, some of the females may not be interested either. In this case, as in all speech preparation, adjustment of the topic must be made to create relevance to the listeners. One way to include the traditional males and the uninterested females is to avoid discussing the "how-to's" of cross-stitching since you have already established several in the audience who don't want to learn the art for themselves. Instead, the speaker might suggest that kits are available as gifts for friends and relatives. Such a gift might be unique for birthdays, Christmas, Chanukah, Mother's Day, and other special days for that person who likes sewing crafts. A discussion of beginners' kits, basic instructions, cost, location, and different styles would be appropriate, along with visuals showing the variations in complexity.

The importance here is in analyzing the audience in order to provide the best angle to a topic and the best wording. Making an assumption that traditional sex roles are present is a mistake. For example, if a male speaker begins a speech on basic car care with the assumption that the females don't know how to care for a car and need to be told, he may offend several females who do know basic mechanics. In fact, I know a female who trains beginning troubleshooters in all aspects of Ford engines. She says 99.9% of her classes are male and that she has experienced much hostility at the beginning of her course. An appropriate topic for her might be how to deal with hostile behavior and overcome sex-role stereotyping.

Select Non-Offensive Language

One way to overcome stereotyping is to carefully select language that avoids showing sexual, racial, religious, or ethnic prejudice.

In the past whenever a singular personal pronoun was used in a general sense, common practice was to choose the masculine pronouns *he, his, him*. In recent times many have realized that this practice is sexist. The following sentence is an example: "When a lawyer finally wins **his** first case, **he** has reason to love the laws of the land." Notice the stereotypical assumption that the lawyer must surely be a male. Today's usage would suggest using the phrase *his or her* and *he or she*. But at times this practice is awkward, especially in speech. The way to avoid the awkwardness is when the sex is unknown, create a plural pronoun situation whenever possible. Changing the above sentence to a plural eliminates the problem: "When lawyers finally win **their** first case, **they** have reason to love the laws of the land."

Gloria Steinem addresses this issue by reversing sexist language in a such a way that the offensiveness is easier to understand:

> Many women feel invisible or aberrant when they are subsumed under a masculine term that is supposed to be universal; yet they are often made to feel trivial and nit-picking if they object. But look at it this way: Would a man feel included in "womankind"? Would he refer to himself as "chairwoman," Congresswoman," or "Mr. Mary Smith"? If a male student earned a "Spinster of Arts" degree, a "Mistress of Science," . . . would he feel equal in academia?[2]

Besides words that indicate sexual stereotyping, there are also words and phrases that indicate a prejudice against other minorities. They should always be avoided.

1. She's quite a broad.
2. He's a typical male.

 3. They Jewed down the prices.
 4. They were Indian givers.
 5. They acted like a pack of Indians.
 6. His actions are effeminate.
 7. Her actions are masculine.
 8. She looked like a dyke.
 9. He looked like a faggot.
10. A black attorney won the case.
11. She is a black novelist.

Again Gloria Steinem addresses the issue of language that belittles according to race and religion.

> If titles like "novelist" and "engineer" were perceived as black unless otherwise stated—if "white novelist" or "white engineer" were necessary qualifiers—would whites feel equal ownership of those professions? If political issues put forward by white male citizens were called "special interest" and those of women and people of color who are the majority were the mainstream, who would feel themselves marginalized? If white people were defined in the negative as nonblack," or Christians were defined as "non-Jews," who would see themselves as the norm of society?[3]

As a speaker, you must learn to be language-conscious. Be aware of prejudices creeping into "common" words and phrases and realize that it is offensive and harms communication.

As you choose a topic that interests you, revise that topic based on audience analysis, and then carefully choose language appropriate to the occasion, you will be on your way to becoming an effective speaker. The next step shows you how to find outside information about your topic and is covered in the next chapter.

Notes

1. James Naismith, *Basketball: Its Origin and Development*, Association Press, New York, 1941. (This book is by the man who created the sport.)
2. Gloria Steinem, *Revolution From Within*, Little, Brown, Boston, 1992, p. 185.
3. Gloria Steinem, *Revolution From Within*, p. 185.

5 Researching Your Topic Learning the Library

Since not only your interest in the topic is vital but also your listeners' interest, making the topic relevant to them is made easier if you know how to use the library.

For the past several years, when I have asked each of my speech classes if they use the library, I have discovered that many of them go in it to study but that 75 to 100 percent do not know how to find magazine articles on a topic. This is similar to getting a new car and only being able to sit in it because you have no idea how to drive it.

The Library Will Be Invaluable Throughout Your Life

Many students believe that the library will be useful only while they are in college and then never again. Not dispelling this illusion is one of the biggest downfalls of our education system. The library is filled with information that, in all likelihood, could have greatly helped you in the past, if you had only known it.

For example, if you have bought a stereo or CD player for your home or your car, you could have easily compared several different models, their features, and their prices—if you had known how easy it is to look up the information in the library. If you want to buy a used car and do not know if the price is really a good one, did you know you can find the average price for that car in the library? Are you going to interview for a job you really want but would like to know a little more about the business? Various kinds of information about businesses throughout the United States (and world) is abundant in the library. And you do not always have to know exactly where in the library the information is. That is the job of librarians; they have gone through school to learn the variety of information possible in a library and where to most easily find it. Their purpose is to help you and to answer questions—that is, if you are willing to ask.

Using the Library Will Save You Hours of Speech Preparation

Even if you have knowledge about your topic, it is still a good idea to check some magazine articles because they can give you a new perspective on it. Somebody else probably already had some great ideas on how to present your topic to a general audience, just the type of audience you have. So why not take advantage of their work and use it to make your work simpler and to add support to your ideas.

First let me indicate that though you may know how to use a card catalog (or the computer version of it), which sends you to books, I am not advocating that you use only books for your information. The problem with books is that you do not have time to read several before your speech is due. So I do not encourage beginning speakers to go only to books. You often can get a wider variety of ideas in a short amount of time from magazine articles, since they are usually only a few pages long.

Learn How to Get to Magazine Articles on Your Topic

So how do you get to these articles? You look in some huge hard-bound books called indexes or reference books (they are called both).

These are in the reference section of any library. They are usually on tables and look like huge encyclopedia sets. Just as an encyclopedia is several volumes, so is each set of indexes. And just as there are several different names of encyclopedias, like *Encyclopedia Britannica, Encyclopedia Americana, World Book Encyclopedia,* and *Collier's Encyclopedia,* the different index sets have different names. The reason for the different titles for the indexes is that they contain references to differing types of topics. That is, some indexes or reference books list magazine articles contained in technical magazines about the sciences, while others contain topics about business, about education, about medicine, and so forth. It is important that you realize the actual magazine articles are not contained in these indexes; rather these reference books list the names of the magazines and the titles of the articles on a wide variety of topics. This listing of titles is why these books are called "indexes" (they index titles) or why they are sometimes called *reference books* (they "refer" you to magazines containing articles on your topic. Below is a listing of a few of the most basic indexes and the types of magazine articles they will lead you to. The title of the index is frequently a key to the types of topics and magazines that are covered.

APPLIED SCIENCE AND TECHNOLOGY INDEX. Topics such as atmosphere, cholesterol, electrodes, fiber optics, soil, and X rays. A variety of topics from A to Z on science and technology.

ARTICLES ON AMERICAN LITERATURE. Topics on any aspect of American literature from its beginnings to the present day.

BIOGRAPHY INDEX. Information about the lives of famous people, past as well as present.

BUSINESS PERIODICALS INDEX. Topics from a wide spectrum of business, such as accounting, arbitration, industries, taxes, medical equipment, wiretapping, women as consumers.

CUMULATIVE INDEX TO NURSING LITERATURE. Topics ranging from accident prevention and nutrition to Y chromosomes.

CURRENT INDEX TO JOURNALS IN EDUCATION. Topics of a wide variety, including listings such as alcoholism or X-rated movies.

HUMANITIES INDEX (used to be INTERNATIONAL INDEX). Topics from anthropology to zoology.

INDEX TO DENTAL LITERATURE. Topics on any aspect of dentistry, such as dental care of the handicapped and root canals.

SOCIAL SCIENCES INDEX. Topics ranging from alcoholism in American Indians to a topic as broad as "youth."

READERS' GUIDE TO PERIODICAL LITERATURE. Topics with a broad
range of appeal, such as abortion, wood carving, and zoology. Indexes common magazines, not technical.

Learn How to Use
Magazine Indexes/Bibliographies

Let's look at sample listings from the *Readers' Guide to Periodical
Literature,* since this is the one most of you will be looking in to find
information on general topics. This index lists the titles of all magazine
articles published for any given year in the type of magazine you can
buy from a bookstore, grocery, or drug store. In other words, the magazines are of a nontechnical nature. To discover which magazines this
index includes, look inside the front cover, where all magazines indexed by this book are listed alphabetically. All indexes have this feature. Since this index lists the articles according to topics, let's gain
some experience by pretending our topic is adult illiteracy.

The first thing you would do after you find the *Reader's Guide* is to
look at the spine of the book and note that each volume has months
and years listed. All articles published in the listed magazines during
this period of time are indexed inside the respective volume. Let's
assume we need the most current information about our topic, we
should go to the most current year. For the most current months, you
will find the index is in paperback and has not yet been put together
into a huge hardbound volume.

When we open the book, we see it is arranged alphabetically by
subject matter, so we turn to the *I*'s and look for the subject of *illiteracy,*
the key word of our topic. Part of the page looks something like the
following, except that the actual index is in very small print.

ILLINOIS CENTRAL TRANSPORTATION COMPANY
Think small and grow. il *Forbes* 142:36-7 D. 12 '88
ILLITERACY See Literacy
ILLNESS See Sickness
ILLUMINATION See Lighting

Next to the topic of *illiteracy* are the words "See Literacy." Whenever
a topic is followed by "See," the index is telling you to look under the

new topic (or topics) where the listing of articles is more likely to occur. So now we go to the "L" section and find the following:

LITERACY
See also
Cultural literacy
Reading
Illiteracy in America L. Lin *Seventeen* 47:98 Ap '88
Education for women . . . a way to equity (health and nutrition atlas) il maps *World Health* p. 18-21 My '88
LITERACY EDUCATION
See also
Comprehensive Competencies Program
Literacy Volunteers of America
Literacy Volunteers of New York City
San Francisco Renaissance (Firm)
ABC's of courage (condensed from Cheeseburgers) B. Greene il *Reader's Digest* 133:126-8 Ag '88
Business fights illiteracy *The Futurist* 22:50 My/Je '88
The crusade against illiteracy (work of B. Bush; cover story) J. E. Harr il *The Saturday Evening Post* 260:42-8 D '88

There are many more articles listed under the subject of literacy, but let's take only the above and learn how to read the abbreviated information the index uses.

The first important piece of information is that we can look under two other subject headings (Cultural Literacy or Reading) and perhaps find other articles. Under the subject "Literacy Education," we could look under four other areas (this listing is under "See also") and check for articles.

Now let's look at the articles provided under "Literacy Education." In the first entry, you know it is an article title because it is indented only three spaces and because of the additional information provided:

1. The first thing listed is always the article title. In this case, the article is titled "ABC's of Courage." Note that the first letter of each word is not capitalized as we would normally do in our writing. The index simplifies and abbreviates words we normally would not.

DO-IT EXERCISE

There are four "LITERACY" entries in addition to the one explained. Answer the following questions about them.

1. What is the title of the article by L. Lin?
2. Who is the author of "The Crusade Against Illiteracy"?
3. What magazine is the article "Business Fights Illiteracy" in?
4. What are the page numbers for "The Crusade Against Illiteracy"?
5. If we were to use the article from *The Saturday Evening Post*, which issue of the magazine do we need?

ANSWERS TO "DO-IT EXERCISE"

1. "Illiteracy in America" (listed under the topic Literacy)
2. J. E. Harr (the last entry listed)
3. *The Futurist* (listed under the topic Literacy Education)
4. Pages 42 through 48 (the next to last entry listed)
5. December 1988 (the last entry listed)

2. Sometimes additional information is given after the title in brackets or parentheses. In this instance, this article is a condensed version of an article originally published in a book called *Cheeseburgers* by B. Greene.

3. After the title of the article is the name of the author. The first letter of the first name is given, and sometimes the initial of the middle name, and then the full spelling of the last name. So the author's name is B. Greene.

4. After the author's name will be, in italics, the name of the magazine where you can find the article. Sometimes before the name of the magazine you will see the small case letters "il." This means that the magazine is illustrated; pictures might become very valuable for a speaker who needs some visual aids, providing they are large enough for the audience to see. Sometimes the name of the

magazine is abbreviated, but at the front of each index is an alphabetical listing of all magazine abbreviations used. This time the full name is given; the name of the magazine is *Reader's Digest*.

5. Then after the magazine name are some numbers. The first number before the colon refers to the volume number of the magazine. Most of the time you can ignore that number. You do not need it. But remember that you definitely need the numbers that go after the colon; these are the pages of the article. Hence, for this article, you need to look on pages 126-128. Also now you know the length of the article, only three pages.

6. The last item in each entry is the date of the magazine. Again months are abbreviated in a simplified way in order to save space. In fact, months that we do not normally abbreviate have abbreviations in the indexes. We now know to find the August 1988 issue of *Reader's Digest*.

Write Each Magazine Article on a Single Index Card

When you begin writing down entries for your topic, you will have a tendency to go in the library with your tablet and write down a list of articles on a sheet of paper. Let me forewarn you that this will complicate your search later on.

The easiest way you can help yourself occurs before you walk in the library. Go to the bookstore or some discount store and buy a package of 3 × 5 index cards. Then you can go to the library and look up your topic. As you find an article title you are interested in pursuing, write all the information about it down on a single card. When you find another article, write that information on a separate card. Each individual article should have its own separate card.

Using separate cards for each article saves time and energy. You need to check to see if your library carries the particular magazine that the article is in. Usually libraries have a book that alphabetically lists which magazines they carry. Now with each entry on a separate card, you can arrange your cards in order so that they are alphabetical accord-

ing to magazine titles. Then all you have to do is go to the library
listing and place a word in the corner of the index card that says either
"yes" (the library subscribes to the magazine) or "no" (the library
doesn't subscribe to it). You can then separate the cards into two piles,
one that you will work with in this particular library because it carries
the magazine you need and one that you will use later to check other
libraries or will toss out. Now, you can go look up the articles. Also,
since libraries arrange their magazines in alphabetical order, your
ability to shuffle the cards alphabetically as you find new titles saves
you from running back and forth between the same magazines. For
example, you can get all the *Newsweeks* at once and all the *Parents*
magazines while you are where they are stacked, and so on. In addition, by having the information on index cards, you can again mark
each separate card as saying the library has this particular issue of the
magazine or the magazine is checked out. Now you can again separate
the cards used (the magazines you have found) from the ones not used
(those you still must find).

If you had listed all your articles on a single sheet of paper, you
would have notes written all over it, and your page would be illegible.
Furthermore, listing on a sheet of paper does not allow you to arrange
the titles of the magazines in alphabetical order or to arrange in piles
of which magazines you found and which you still have to find.

Magazine Articles
Are Sometimes on Microfilm

Since libraries have a limited amount of space to store their collec-
tion of books and magazines, they seldom have room for actual hard
copies of magazines more than five years old. In order to provide the
researcher access to past issues, many libraries have magazines on
microfilm, a roll of film (much like what you would put in your camera) that must be put on a microfilm machine in order to read it. All
magazines on microfilm are usually located in one area, frequently in
boxes inside drawers or stacked in revolving racks. The boxes are

labeled with the title and the months and years of the magazine included on that particular film.

Most machines have directions right on them, but anyone who has never used one is encouraged to request help from a librarian, who is eager to show a patron how to turn on the machine, thread the film, and fast-forward it to the desired article. The machine has a monitor, just like a computer screen, that shows the respective pages of the magazine. In addition, most machines have a button labeled "print" and a coin slot for a dime. By dropping in your coin and pushing the print button, you receive a copy of the page on the screen. So you do have a chance to get a hard copy of any pages you want.

Some Libraries Now Have Computers to Help You Find Articles

The most current innovation in searching for both magazines and books derives from the technology of the computer.

Some libraries now have what is called *on-line searching*, a term meaning a computerized search. One computer or series of computers has a program in them that searches for books on given topics. A different computer searches for magazine articles. We will concentrate on the one leading us to magazines.

There is a keyboard, similar to a typewriter, and a screen. When you sit at the screen, instructions usually tell you to push the keyboard button labeled "enter" to begin the search. Then instructions to enter your subject or topic appear, so you type in your topic. If you were to research the topic discussed in Chapters 2 and 4, you would type in "basketball" and then press the enter key.

The computer takes a moment to run the search; when it is finished, the display on the screen has the same setup as the page that you saw previously from the *Reader's Guide*. The following is a sample of what would appear on the computer screen if you typed in the topic "basketball."

FIRST SCREEN AFTER YOU TYPE "BASKETBALL" AND PRESS ENTER

InfoTrac EF	Expanded Academic Index	Subject Guide
Subjects containing the words: BASKETBALL		Rec.'s
Basketball		253
(48) subdivisions		
(3) related subjects		
Basketball (college)		555
(46) subdivisions		
Basketball (professional)		328
(42) subdivisions		
Basketball Clubs		231
(32) subdivisions		
Basketball Coaches		264
(46) subdivisions		
Basketball Coaching		63
(6) subdivisions		
Basketball For Women		76
(24) subdivisions		
Basketball Players		680

This is all that fits on a single screen, but there are still many other subjects about basketball. To view additional topics that are not in your view, you push the down arrow key. For those of you who are intimidated by the keyboard, further instructions follow. One area on your keyboard, usually the lower right, will have four keys in close proximity, each having an arrow pointing to either the left, the right, up, or down. You will notice that on the screen there is a highlighted area. By pushing the down arrow, you move the highlighted area down to the topic you desire. As you continue to press the down arrow, it will highlight the last topic "Basketball Players." Press down again and a new topic you couldn't see before scrolls onto the lower screen. If you hold the arrow down, the new topics will scroll up the screen at a steady pace, and you will see some of the following.

SECOND SCREEN AS YOU CONTINUE TO PUSH DOWN ARROW KEY

Afro-American Basketball Players
McDonald's Basketball Open
National Basketball Associations All-Star Game
Wheelchair Basketball
Women Basketball Players

Look back at the first screen you would see if you entered the topic "basketball"; under the first heading in parentheses is an indication that there are 48 subdivisions on basketball. As a speaker, this means that you can look at those subdivisions to see if any would interest both you and your audience. In order to see some of your options, you merely push the up arrow key until you are back to the top of the first screen. When "(48) subdivisions" is highlighted, press the enter key and watch the screen. You will see an alphabetical listing of possible topic choices. The following is a sample screen of some of them; remember all of these subdivisions are related to your larger heading "basketball." This list will continue as you press the down arrow key and until all 253 subdivisions are listed.

SCREEN DISPLAY AFTER YOU HIGHLIGHT "(48) subdivisions"
UNDER FIRST ENTRY ON THE FIRST SCREEN AND PRESS ENTER

—accidents
—achievements and awards
—africa
—analysis
—anecdotes, cartoons, satire, etc.
—appreciation
—commemorative coins, stamps, etc.
—competitions
—computer programs
—corrupt practices
—defense
—draft
—economic aspects
—equipment and supplies
—fans
—history

Now let's suppose that you thought the second screen above had a potentially interesting topic: "Wheelchair Basketball." When you see any topic that you'd like to have some magazine articles on, you highlight that topic and press the enter key. If you highlighted the above topic and pressed enter, here is the screen you would likely see.

SCREEN DISPLAY AFTER TOPIC "Wheelchair Basketball"
IS HIGHLIGHTED AND THE ENTER KEY PRESSED

1   Comparison of mood states of college able-bodied and wheelchair basketball players, Patricia Paulsen, Ron French and Claudine Sherrill, Perceptual and Motor Skills, Oct 1991 v73 n2 p396 (3).
             Press Enter for abstract.

2   The rabbi of roundball; Reeve Brenner has developed a game that allows the able-bodied and the disabled to compete on a basis of equality. (new version of basketball) (Games) Ed Miller, Sports Illustrated, July 1, 1991 v75 n1 p6(2).

3   The stuff of champions. (disabled athletes Randy Snow, Ben Hunter, Doug Kennedy) by Dianne Young il v25 Southern Living Sept '90 p119(3)

4   Sat down for life by fate, former basketball star Landon Turner rebounds with a gritty comeback. by Pete Axthelm il v31 People Weekly Feb 13 '89 p61(2)

The screen lists various magazine articles on whatever topic you highlight and press the enter key for. The listing is in a format similar to that of the hardbound indexes we already learned about, with the exception that the first page number of the article is listed at the end. The number that follows in parentheses tells exactly how many pages in the article.

An advantage of this computerized system is that it is fast and searches many different indexes, whereas you would have to move from index to index to look up the information in the bound volumes.

A second advantage is that often you can print whatever you see on the computer screen. There is usually a key on your keyboard labeled "print" or else the screen has instructions about which key to push to get a printout. If the computer is already hooked up to a printer and you push the print key, the printer types whatever is on your computer screen. That means that you do not have to write down the list of articles you are interested in, but rather the printer will print them for you.

Different libraries may have differing instructions for computer searches, but usually you will see step-by-step instructions on the screen, or a librarian will demonstrate how to perform a search for articles. Librarians are eager to show off their computerized systems, so if you fear the computer or are hesitant to attempt a new program, ask your librarian for assistance.

The two disadvantages of the computerized system are that it has not yet indexed articles more than a few years old, so if you want to do a historical search or look at the past, you may still need to go to the separate bound indexes. Furthermore, the printout from the screen is on a single sheet of paper, lacking the advantages of the index cards. Sometimes, if I am doing long-term research and have many magazines, I will cut the entries and place them on large index cards so I can ultimately save time by making separate notes and alphabetizing the cards as needed. Both the hardbound indexes and the computer searches provide a wealth of information for anyone who cares to look.

The library is the speaker's greatest friend. Within it are thousands of articles, as well as books, on any given topic. Hence, your topic has already been researched by different people, many of them experts. You can discover interesting facets to your topic that you never knew existed. You will be introduced to a variety of subtopics that you haven't thought about before. You can get ideas for getting the attention of the audience. You can use anecdotes and stories for the body of your speech, as long as you indicate your source. You will be able to gain credibility because of your reading. All of this is possible when you learn to use the library effectively.

6 Organizing Your Topic

You would not go on a vacation without planning it first, and if you were planning one, you would first think of possible places you would like to go and then choose one. You would also decide how long it would take you to get there, what route to take, where to stay on the way, and where to stay and what to do after your arrival. Planning is necessary in several areas of life. For example, if you decided to build a deck onto your home, you could not start construction without deciding where it will be in relation to the rest of the house, what size and shape will look best, what material you want it to be made of, and how much money it will cost.

Speech preparation is no different from other facets of life. In order to get the desired end product, you must plan the steps to get to your finished speech.

Work on Speech Preparation in Steps

Go back to the speech schedule at the end of Chapter 1 and notice the seven steps. Remember to break down your preparation into these steps and tackle each one, checking each off as you accomplish it.

When you break down a task, it becomes more manageable, like a road map to a destination.

So far, you have accomplished Step 1 (choosing a topic appropriate to the audience) and Step 2 (reading about the topic) of your seven-day schedule.

You are now ready for Step 3: setting up the organization for the body of the speech, which is possible because you have done your library research and your reading about the topic.

How to Use the First Reading of the Articles

After you have used the library and found the articles on your topic, you will read them **without** taking notes. Beginners usually express disbelief at such a notion. But if you follow this advice, you will save considerable time. After you finish this chapter, you will understand why.

The first reading of the articles gives you an idea of how various individuals, most of whom are experts, approach your topic. The most that you will write down will be one or two sentences **on your note card** about the main ideas discussed in the article so that, at a glance, you will recall the article.

The purpose of reading the articles is to see how the authors subdivide the topic, to discover what main ideas are repeated in different articles, and to gain from this information how YOU want to organize your own topic for your speech.

It is from the initial reading that you will learn which articles to discard and which to reread more thoroughly. If you take thorough notes on all the articles the **first** time you read them, you will have taken lots of notes you will never need from articles you will never use, and thus hours of your time will be wasted because you will throw away much you have written.

Combine What You Know With What You Have Read

Now go back to that sheet of paper when you first selected your topic—the one where you sat for fifteen minutes and wrote all you could about the topic. Which ideas or questions that you wrote were discussed in the articles you read? Which articles did you find the most interesting? Those may be the same ideas about the topic that your audience will find interesting. One of the important purposes of reading is to discover interesting facets of your topic you haven't thought about before. These readings help you discover what the **audience** will find interesting, thus fulfilling a major obligation of you as a public speaker.

Next, make a list of main ideas about your topic. If you are demonstrating or showing how to do something, make a list of the large steps involved in completing it.

Write a Thesis Statement Only One Sentence Long

Your ultimate task is to pick two, three, or four main ideas for your speech and place them within one sentence. Doing this creates a thesis statement: one sentence explaining the two, three, or four main subdivisions for the body of your speech. This organization gives you a framework so you will know what to support, and ultimately, the thesis **prepares your audience** in advance for what you will be discussing in the body of the speech.

Whether you are merely informing about a process or actually demonstrating that process, your job is to cite only three or four main points or large steps in a single-sentence thesis statement. These main ideas or steps are the most important part of your speech because they are what you want your audience to remember. The number of points you are going to announce results from your research, your reading of the articles. So you cannot know what main ideas to use for the body of the speech until you have acquired enough knowledge about your topic.

Research has shown time and time again that an audience cannot remember very many main ideas. In fact, though the percentages vary a little, most of the testing indicates that audiences remember one fourth or less of what they hear. David Peoples, international speaker and sales trainer, indicates that listeners remember only 20 percent of what they hear.[1] As a result of the prevalence of poor listening, many established speakers prefer to use the **KISS** method of organization: **Keep It Simple, Speaker.** In other words, an effective speaker is one who simplifies for the sake of the audience. This simplification is hard work, and the task is made easier when a limited number of main ideas are presented. Most experts suggest from two to seven main points. Some suggest no more than five. In fact, Hillary Rodman Clinton, attorney and wife of President Clinton, helps with her husband's speeches and is one "who can convince him it's better to make three points in a speech than six."[2] For a four- to six-minute speech, the maximum possible to support with details would probably be three points, and some speakers might choose only two in order to add ample supporting details.

This organization makes the job at hand easier for both the speaker and the listener. It is easier for you as a speaker because you have provided yourself a framework to follow. Those parts of magazine articles that do not support the framework or subdivisions of the body are discarded; the details that do explain, amplify, and illustrate the subdivisions are slotted under the main idea supported. In other words, you have given yourself clear guidelines to follow. And these guidelines make the listener's job easier, too. Since listeners forget most of what they hear, the more clearly organized the speaker is, the easier it is to follow and remember main ideas.

For example, if I were to announce the following list of letters to an audience and ask them to repeat them back immediately in order, probably no one could: H, B, F, C, E, A, G, D. But if I announce these same letters in a more organized way (such as, A, B, C, D, E, F, G, H), most of the audience would be able to repeat them in order.

The simplified organization makes it easy to remember. Organize your speech **simply for your audience** so that they will easily remember your main ideas.

Your research and knowledge will determine what organization you choose. For example, let's suppose you picked the "history of basketball" as a potential topic. You chose this subtopic of basketball because it was listed on the computer screen when you were previewing the 48 listings under the major heading of "basketball." When you highlight the subtopic "history" and press enter, you have a listing of lots of articles on the subject. So you print the articles that look the most interesting and look them up and read them. As you read you discover the interesting story behind the creation of basketball as an American sport, you discover the amazing rules of the original game, and you discover when the first paycheck for the sport came into being and how the sport progressed into a major league game. You may have discovered several other interesting facts about the original clothing and how it has evolved, about the first women's basketball team (and a totally different set of rules), about competitions and injuries, and on and on. After reading several articles, you are the one who decides which facts from these articles (1) will be most interesting to your listeners, (2) which of those facts can be slotted into a large category or subdivision, and (3) how many categories you have time to support with details in the time allotted you. In other words, you decide which facts are most similar and can be lumped together under a heading that you create. Eventually each heading will represent one subdivision of the body of the speech. As stated before, you will likely have from two to four subdivisions in the body of a 4- to 6-minute speech.

For this topic of the history of basketball, we might find that our most interesting material could be categorized under two headings that have enough detail to be a 5-minute speech: how it was created and what its original rules were.

Making a Topic Easy to Follow Is Hard Work

The subdivisions from the body of your speech are what makes up the single organizing sentence called a thesis, which is stated by you as the last sentence of the introduction of the speech and which acts as a signal of what is to come. For example, the thesis for our basketball topic might be "Basketball is truly an American sport with an interesting past as you will see when I tell you about its creation and its unusual rules." Then **only** those facts that give details explaining each subdivision are used; the other facts are discarded if they do not specifically support one of the subdivisions.

This care for matching details to main ideas is true for any topic you have chosen and have organized around a thesis. Later in this chapter you will see a series of five thesis statements on a variety of topics. The organization stated within the thesis determines the supporting detail. That way the speaker knows to eliminate details that do not amplify, explain, or prove the main idea. The thesis helps both the speaker and the audience.

Let's take a look at how to organize a list of facts. The following is a listing of facts about potbelly pigs from a past speech; the problem with them is that they are not organized under main headings. First let's look at the facts in the order they were presented.

   I. Potbelly pigs arrived in the U.S. in 1985.
     A. Keith & Connie imported twenty potbellies.
     B. The U.S. has the largest population, which is 36,000.
  II. When picking your potbelly, make sure you see both parents.
     A. Parents are indication of size.
     B. Some pigs claiming to be potbellies are not because the breeding to larger pigs has created much too large a pig.
       1. Large pigs will be unmanageable.
       2. You can't possibly know whether it will grow too large without seeing the parents, so do not underestimate the importance.
 III. Feeding your pig is basically the same as feeding any other pets.
 IV. A bed for the pig should be established.
     A. He will know that his bed is where he sleeps.
     B. You should keep your potbelly in its bed whenever unsupervised.
       1. If left alone the potbelly might mess on the floor or carpet.
       2. It might chew on some furniture or shoe or some other item and destroy it.
  V. A potbelly needs to be groomed regularly.
 VI. Potbellies are very easily trained.
     A. They are the fourth smartest creature.
     B. They can do tricks.

Each roman numeral should indicate a main idea in the body of the speech, but there are some problems. First of all, there are too many main ideas for a five-minute speech. Secondly, the facts are listed randomly without taking similar facts, grouping them together, and creating a main heading for them; the way the facts are currently presented makes it much harder for the audience to retain the information.

Let's redo the organization from the facts we have. Remember that each roman numeral is a main idea or subdivision in the body of the speech; also remember that each subdivision is to have details that further support and explain it. The first roman numeral for the above speech merely states a year the pigs arrived in America; though a source needs to be cited for this fact, the point is that the sentence isn't a main idea (that is, a generalization) but rather a fact that cannot have much more support. It would be better to have as the main idea a broader generalization such as the **"history"** or **"importation"** and then cite various facts that further explain and amplify the broad generalization. The second roman numeral is also too narrow; all the supporting details are about things a buyer should know when **"selecting"** a potbelly; roman numeral II and everything underneath will support this broad category, though additional specifics need to be added. For example, what size should a full-grown potbelly be— what weight and what length? It would be very beneficial to have some visuals so the audience can see what a full-grown one is to look like. What colors are they? Visuals help audience interest and retention. Further facts the audience would likely be interested in are the price range when purchasing a potbelly and where to go to buy one.

Now look at roman numerals III, IV, and V. All this information could be grouped under the single main subdivision of **"care."** Then underneath this subdivision a discussion of feeding, bedding, and grooming. In fact, the "feeding" area is not detailed and needs details added, such as what size bowl, what kind of food, where do you get it, how much do you feed, how many times a day, and how much does it cost. Do you leave water out all the time, or do you take it up so the pig won't slosh around in it and upset it? Also, the facts about the bed need to be more detailed. Remember the reporters' questions we applied to cars in Chapter 2? We need to use them here. For example what size of a bed is needed? What should it be made of? Should there be a pad or pillow to soften the bed, or will the potbelly eat the padding? Are there instances the speaker can cite that tell the story of a pet potbelly not being crated when left alone and then destroying some property? Detailed stories of actual happenings help retain audience interest. In addition, the listener needs to know what grooming is needed. Do potbellies get bathed? How? With what kind of soap? How often? Do they need to be trimmed? Do their hooves need to be trimmed? Do they need vet checkups like a dog or cat? Do they tend to get any illnesses? Specific details answer questions the audience would naturally have about the subdivision.

The last roman numeral is on **"training,"** and this subdivision is general enough to leave as it is. Again, the problem is with the specific details—there are none. Can a potbelly be housebroken? If so, how is this feat accomplished? What kind of tricks can a potbelly be trained to do? How does an owner go about training one? And if a claim is made that they are the fourth smartest creature, where does it come from? The source must be cited because this is not common knowledge.

Now that we can see how to make simpler and more accurate subdivisions for the body and now that we realize some more facts are necessary for the supporting details underneath the general headings, we can also begin to grasp that there will not be time for all this information within the five minutes allotted. Therefore, some items need to be eliminated. It is better to eliminate one or two of the general subdivisions than it is to eliminate the details necessary to support, amplify, and explain a subdivision. Therefore, we could have as the new thesis, "A potbelly pig can be an excellent pet as long as you understand the importance of **selecting, caring** for, and **training** one." History seems the least interesting and the least supported, so it could be eliminated altogether. The new outline follows. Compare this outline to the previous one.

I. A potbelly pig can be an excellent pet as long as you understand the importance of properly **selecting** one.

   A. Check the parents for size.

   B. Know the proper full-grown size of a potbelly.

   (Show picture of potbelly and explain)

      1. Tell proper weight range.

      2. Tell approximate length.

      3. Tell about colors.

   C. Tell the range of prices for one.

   D. Tell where to buy one.

II. Now that you know how best to select a potbelly, you need to understand how to **care** for one properly.

   A. The first aspect of proper care is feeding. The way to a potbelly's heart is through its stomach, and feeding one is similar to feeding any common pet.

      1. Tell size of bowl and type of food.

      2. Tell where to find food and how much to feed.

      3. Tell cost of feeding.

      4. Explain watering.

   B. Further **care** for the potbelly involves necessary bedding.

      1. Tell bed size and construction (use visual aid).

      2. Discuss problems if potbelly is left alone to roam while the owner is out. Cite story.

   C. Now that the necessary food and shelter have been provided for our unusual pet, we need to discuss the needed grooming.

      1. Discuss bathing.

      2. Discuss health checks.

III. So far we have learned to pick a good potbelly and properly care for it; now let's add an area that often surprises those who do not know about this pet—**training.**

   A. Discuss intelligence and cite source for information.

   B. Tell how to housebreak.

   C. Cite tricks a potbelly can learn.

All of the outline above will provide the body of the speech, and it is this kind of detailed outlining that encourages good extemporaneous delivery. If three subdivisions become too long for a five-minute speech, then narrow it to two. Which two you choose depends on you and what you believe will be the most educational and interesting to your audience.

Creating a thesis is the most important part of your speech, for it is this single sentence that prepares the audience for what follows in the body, as well as provides you guidelines for creating the introduction and conclusion. In other words, the body is usually created first—and then the introduction and conclusion. The speaker prepares a listing of facts and then figures how to group them; the grouping is announced to the listener as a main idea or subdivision. As a speaker, you must not assume it is the listener's responsibility to figure out your organization. You, the speaker, have the responsibility to make what you say easy to comprehend through providing a clear statement of the organizational pattern you will follow in the body. The statement that achieves this announcement of main ideas to be followed in the body is called the thesis.

Rewrite the Thesis to Get the Best Wording Possible

Rarely, if ever, will a speaker actually use the first main ideas that come to mind. Even if the initial ideas are used, it takes reworking the wording to make the thesis statement into one simple sentence.

Let's learn the process of analyzing thesis statements by finding and correcting weaknesses in each of the following ones. These are based on the assumption that the speaker has a list of facts and is creating the main subdivisions and grouping details underneath.

1. Most plane crashes result from several possible causes, such as air-traffic control systems, human errors, engine failure, maintenance problems, warning-system failure, bad weather, or birds.
2. Drywall repair is simple if you remember the right tools, remove the damaged area, patch the hole, and seal the cracks.
3. Cholesterol can be understood by learning what it is, the risk factors involved, which foods you should avoid, and which foods you should eat.
4. The effects of stress are bodily effects, ineffective behavior, and upsetting thoughts.
5. If you are considering buying a new car, you should know the definition of the lemon law, the steps you take, and the dealer's obligations.

Let's look at each example.

Original Thesis #1

Most plane crashes result from several possible causes, such as air-traffic control systems, human errors, engine failure, maintenance problems, warning-system failure, bad weather, or birds.

In the first thesis on plane crashes, the major problem is that seven main ideas are too many for any audience to remember, especially when the thesis could be shortened by combining some into a larger category. For example, "air-traffic control systems," "engine failure," and "warning systems" all involve machinery; the area of "maintenance problems" could easily fall under the other area of "human errors," and "weather" and "birds" are environmental problems. Therefore, by working some more with the thesis, the speaker could make it easier for the audience to remember by shortening the number of subdivisions.

IMPROVEMENT FOR THESIS STATEMENT #1: "Most plane crashes result from human error, machinery malfunction, or environmental hazards."

Original Thesis #2

Drywall repair is simple if you remember the right tools, remove the damaged area, patch the hole, and seal the cracks.

The major problem with the second thesis is that it is aimed toward people who own a home. This topic was, in fact, given to an audience where many did not own any property. Two problems exist. The first problem is that those who own a home or rental may already know this information, so it might not fulfill the obligation of being new. The second problem is that those who do not own property do not need to know how to repair drywall because they have no intention of doing it, so it does not fulfill the obligations of interest or usefulness. If aiming the topic at mostly "prospective" home owners, the speaker could show that drywall repair is quite simple and inexpensive, even for an amateur. In this case, an analysis of the audience is very important, so the speaker can figure how best to approach the topic to interest the audience, while giving them information that is new, useful, and interesting.

IMPROVEMENT FOR THESIS STATEMENT #2: Repairing drywall is easy for anyone if you remember the three letters **T, P,** and **S,** which stand for tool, patch, and seal.

Original Thesis #3

Cholesterol can be understood by learning what it is, the risk factors involved, which foods you should avoid, and which foods you should eat.

This third thesis statement has four subdivisions, and only the last two are parallel in structure. That is, whenever you list the main ideas in your thesis, list them so each has about the same number of words and the same kind of words. For example, the first subdivision above ends in -*ing*. Therefore, the others should also have an -*ing* word, or the first should not. Such parallel structure helps the audience realize these are your main ideas for the body of the speech. You must provide such keys so the audience is prepared for what is to follow.

The wording could be a variety of ways, but a rule for your thesis subdivisions is that they must always be parallel and easy to remember. So we could reword the sentence to say "You can use cholesterol to your advantage by learning the definition, knowing risk factors, avoiding harmful foods, and eating healthful foods." Better yet, we could shorten the sentence more by combining the first two subdivisions. After all, once you say the definition, you are done supporting that particular main idea, so it is a little narrow anyway. The definition and the risk factors explain the different types of cholesterol, so simplify the thesis by combining the two into one. Also, since the first subdivision does not use the word *foods*, the repetition in the last two should be changed. In a thesis where items in a series exist, the items must be parallel with one another in both form and content.

IMPROVEMENT FOR THESIS STATEMENT #3: "You can use cholesterol to your advantage if you understand the different types, avoid harmful eating, and choose healthful foods."

Original Thesis #4

The effects of stress are bodily effects, ineffective behavior, and upsetting thoughts.

The problem with this thesis is that the content of the ideas is not parallel. The word *bodily* has its counterparts, which would be better to use. For example, *bodily* is an adjective, so *behavior* could be changed to *behavioral* with a noun after it. Also the word *effects* is repeated and should not be. So, in rewriting the sentence, we can simplify the wording to "Stress affects a person's body, behavior, and mind." Or we can change it to "The effects of stress are physical, behavioral, and emotional." Or we can change it to a logical sequence of effects by saying, "Stress first affects an individual emotionally, then physically, and lastly, behaviorally."

Or we can change it and create an acronym—a word created from the first letter of a series of words.

IMPROVEMENT FOR THESIS STATEMENT #4: According to the dictionary, the word *ebb* means a decline and is the perfect word to describe how stress negatively affects our emotions, behavior, and body.

Original Thesis #5

> If you are considering buying a new car, you should know the definition of the lemon law, the steps you take, and the dealer's obligations.

Like the others, this thesis needs to be simplified and made more parallel. It is not clear whether the second subdivision, "the steps you take," is for buying the car or using the lemon law. Furthermore, the main ideas are not parallel in form. That is, the first one consists of a noun followed by a prepositional phrase; the second one is a noun followed by a subject and verb; the third is a possessive phrase. All of the subdivisions should be the same form. They are items in a series, and making the series parallel helps the reader realize you are stating your main ideas, your thesis. And parallel structure is easier to remember, for both the speaker and the audience. If we reword this thesis, we can make the listener aware that all subdivisions deal with the lemon law and not just buying a car.

IMPROVEMENT FOR THESIS STATEMENT #5: "Anyone who buys a new car needs to know three things about the 'lemon law': first, the definition of the law; second, the obligations of the buyer; and, third, the requirements of the dealer."

Rewriting the Thesis Is Necessary

There are many ways of rewriting a thesis. The difficult realization for a beginner is to understand that rewriting is vital. There is no such thing as creating the perfectly worded sentence on the first try. The process requires that the writer rework the thesis many times in order to find the best possible wording so the speaker can say it simply and the audience can remember it easily.

After you have a strong thesis statement, you break it into subdivisions for the body and begin supporting each assertion with specific details—our next step in preparing a dynamic speech.

Notes

1. David Peoples, *Presentations Plus,* John Wiley, New York, 1992, pp. 79-80.
2. Margaret Carlson, "All Eyes on Hillary," *Time,* September 14, 1992, p. 33.

7 Supporting Your Thesis

Once you know your thesis, you know the organization for the body of the speech. The main ideas of the thesis provide the large categories that you will support in the body of your speech. *Support* means clarification, explanation, quotations, or demonstration. What you want your audience to remember are your main ideas (your thesis); the supporting detail is to help make these main ideas memorable. The body is the main part of the speech and takes most of the speaker's time, consisting of 75 to 85 percent of the speech. As you move into the body, you will restate each subdivision of the thesis separately and then support it. And you will organize the body in the *exact order* you named the main ideas in the thesis.

Following is an outline of the body for each of the thesis statements from the previous chapter. First look at the thesis, and then note how the body follows its lead.

Thesis 1 divided into individual sections for the body:

    I. Plane crashes result from human error.
    II. Plane crashes result from machinery malfunction.
    III. Plane crashes result from environmental hazards.

Thesis 2 divided into individual sections for the body:

    I. Repairing drywall is easy if you know the tools.
   II. Repairing drywall is easy if you learn to patch.
  III. Repairing drywall is easy if you know how to seal.

Thesis 3 divided into individual sections for the body:

    I. You can use cholesterol to your advantage if you understand the different types.
   II. You can use cholesterol to your advantage if you avoid harmful eating.
  III. You can use cholesterol to your advantage if you choose healthful foods.

Thesis 4 divided into individual sections for the body:

    I. Stress affects our emotions.
   II. Stress affects our behavior.
  III. Stress affects our body.

Thesis 5 divided into individual sections for the body:

    I. Anyone buying a new car needs to know the legal definition of the "Lemon Law."
   II. Anyone buying a new car needs to know the obligations of the buyer when applying the "Lemon Law."
  III. Anyone buying a new car needs to know the requirements of the dealer concerning the "Lemon Law."

Repetition Is a Memory Device

Since you already stated the thesis in the introduction, you do not repeat your whole thesis as one sentence in the body of the speech; rather you repeat only that single subdivision you are going to explain and support. The audience will not remember all the subdivisions from just one announcement of them. So the body gives you an opportunity for repetition of each separate subdivision as a memory aid for your listeners. If your goal is to get them to remember your main ideas, the more times you can say those ideas, the more likely the audience will retain the information after you sit down.

You can realize the truth of this statement by noticing advertisements. Listen to how many times a phone number is repeated on the radio or TV. Notice how many times you see an ad for a given cigarette, food, beverage, or other product. Some have slogans they repeat throughout the year so you **can't** forget. For example, take the quiz below by filling in the blank lines.

**SEE IF YOU CAN FILL IN THE NAME
OF THE ADVERTISED PRODUCT**

1. Please don't squeeze the _____.
2. Don't leave home without it: _____.
3. The breakfast of champions is _____.
4. Just for the taste of it, drink _____.
5. The taste of the new generation is _____.
6. _____ melt in your mouth, not in your hand.
7. _____ soup is good food.
8. Have you driven a _____ lately?
9. The heartbeat of America is _____.
10. Reach out and touch someone: _____.

From my experience in giving this quiz to a wide variety of classes over several years, I have discovered that most students score a perfect 10. And they never even studied for it; they hadn't heard me lecture on the material; they didn't read a text and underline the key slogans. In fact, it was a pop quiz for my students, just like for you. Why do you have these in your memory if you've not even tried to remember them? The answer is one word: REPETITION. Repetition is the key to having your audience remember your topic (and you) when you deliver a speech. (Answers to above quiz: 1. Charmin, 2. American Express, 3. Wheaties, 4. Diet Coke, 5. Pepsi, 6. M & Ms, 7. Campbell's, 8. Ford, 9. Chevrolet, and 10. AT&T.)

One of the greatest speeches of the past century is Martin Luther King, Jr.'s "I Have A Dream." Though the impact of this speech was a result of King's delivery, notice his use of repetition. The speech is provided below; I have highlighted the repetitions to demonstrate King's powerful use of this technique.

I HAVE A DREAM
Martin Luther King, Jr.

I am happy to join with you today in what will go down in history as the greatest demonstration for freedom in the history of our nation.

Five score years ago, a great American, in whose symbolic shadow we stand today, signed the Emancipation Proclamation. This momentous decree came as a great beacon light of hope to millions of Negro slaves, who had been seared in the flames of withering **injustice**. It came as a joyous daybreak to end the long night of their captivity.

But **one hundred years later,** the **Negro** still is not **free. One hundred years later,** the life of the **Negro** is still sadly crippled by the manacles of segregation and the chains of discrimination. **One hundred years later,** the **Negro** lives on a lonely island of poverty in the midst of a vast ocean of material prosperity. **One hundred years later,** the **Negro** is still languished in the corners of American society and finds himself an exile in his own land. And so we've come here today to dramatize a shameful condition.

In a sense we've come to our nation's Capitol to cash a **check.** When the architects of our republic wrote the magnificent words of the Constitution and the Declaration of Independence, they were signing a **promissory note** to which every American was to fall heir. This **note** was a promise that all men—yes, black men as well as white men—would be guaranteed the unalienable rights of life, liberty, and the pursuit of happiness.

It is obvious today that America has defaulted on this **promissory note** insofar as her citizens of color are concerned. Instead of honoring this sacred obligation, America has given the Negro people a **bad check**—a **check** which has come back marked **"insufficient funds."**

But we refuse to believe that the bank of justice is bankrupt. We refuse to believe that there are **insufficient funds** in the great vaults of opportunity of this nations. And so we've come to cash this **check**— a **check** that will give us upon demand the riches of **freedom** and the security of **justice.**

We have also come to this hallowed spot to remind America of the fierce urgency of now. This is no time to engage in the luxury of cooling off or to take the tranquilizing drug of gradualism. **Now is the time** to make real the promises of democracy. **Now is the time** to rise from the dark and desolate valley of segregation to the sunlit path of racial **justice. Now is the time** to lift our nation from the quicksands

of racial **injustice** to the solid rock of brotherhood. Now is the time
to make **justice** a reality for all of **God's children.**

It would be fatal for the nation to overlook the urgency of the
moment. This sweltering summer of the **Negro's** legitimate discontent
will not pass until there is an invigorating autumn of **freedom** and
equality. Nineteen sixty-three is not an end, but a beginning. Those
who hope that the **Negro** needed to blow off steam and will now be
content will have a rude awakening if the nation returns to business
as usual. There will be neither rest nor tranquility in America until the
Negro is granted his citizenship rights. The whirlwinds of revolt will
continue to shake the foundations of our nation until the bright day
of **justice** emerges.

But there is something that I must say to my people, who stand on
the warm threshold which leads into the palace of **justice.** In the process of gaining our rightful place, we must not be guilty of wrongful
deeds. Let us not seek to satisfy our thirst for **freedom** by drinking
from the cup of bitterness and hatred.

We must forever conduct our struggle on the high plane of dignity
and discipline. We must not allow our creative protest to degenerate
into physical violence. Again and again we must rise to the majestic
heights of meeting physical force with soul force.

The marvelous new militancy which has engulfed the **Negro** com-
munity must not lead us to a distrust of all **white** people. For many of
our **white** brothers, as evidenced by their presence here today, **have
come to realize** that their **destiny** is tied up with our **destiny.** They
have come to realize that their **freedom** is inextricably bound to our
freedom. We cannot walk alone.

As we walk, we must make the pledge that we shall always march
ahead. We cannot turn back. There are those who are asking the devo-
tees of civil rights, "When will you be **satisfied?" We can never be satisfied as long as** the **Negro** is the victim of the unspeakable horrors
of police brutality. **We can never be satisfied as long as** our bodies,
heavy with the fatigue of travel, cannot gain lodging in the motels of
the highways and the hotels of the cities. **We cannot be satisfied as
long as** the **Negro's** basic mobility is from a smaller ghetto to a larger
one. **We can never be satisfied as long as** our children are stripped of
their selfhood and robbed of their dignity by signs stating "For
Whites Only." **We cannot be satisfied as long as** a **Negro** in Mississippi cannot vote and a **Negro** in New York believes he has nothing
for which to vote. No, no, we are **not satisfied,** and **we will not be satisfied** until **justice** rolls down like waters, and righteousness like a
mighty stream.

I am not unmindful that **some of you have come here** out of great
trials and tribulations. **Some of you have come** fresh from narrow jail
cells. **Some of you have come** from areas where your quest for **free-**

dom left you battered by the storms of persecution and staggered by the winds of police brutality. You have been the veterans of creative suffering. **Continue to work with the faith that unearned suffering is redemptive.**

Go back to Mississippi, **go back** to Alabama, **go back** to South Carolina, **go back** to Georgia, **go back** to Louisiana, **go back** to the slums and ghettos of our Northern cities, knowing that somehow this situation can and will be changed. Let us not wallow in the valley of despair.

I say to you today, my friends, so even though we face the difficulties of today and tomorrow, I still have a **dream**. It is a **dream** deeply rooted in the American **dream.**

I have a dream that one day this nation will rise up and live out the true meaning of its creed, "We hold these truths to be self-evident, that all men are created equal."

I have a dream that one day on the red hills of Georgia the sons of former slaves and the sons of former slaveowners will be able to sit down together at the table of brotherhood.

I have a dream that one day even the state of Mississippi, a state sweltering with the heat of **injustice,** sweltering with the heat of oppression, will be transformed into an oasis of **freedom** and **justice.**

I have a dream that my four little children will one day live in a nation where they will not be judged by the color of their skin but by the content of their character. **I have a dream** today.

I have a dream that one day, down in Alabama, with its vicious racists, with its governor having his lips dripping with the words of interposition and nullification, one day right there in Alabama little black boys and white girls as sisters and brothers. **I have a dream** today.

I have a dream that one day every valley shall be exalted, every hill and mountain shall be made low, the rough places will be made plane and the crooked places will be made straight, and the glory of the Lord shall be revealed, and all flesh shall see it together.

This is our hope. This is the **faith** that I go back to the South with. With this **faith** we will be able to hew out of the mountain of despair a stone of hope. With this **faith** we will be able to transform the jangling discords of our nations into a beautiful symphony of brotherhood. With this **faith** we will be able to work **together,** to pray **together,** to stand up for **freedom together,** knowing that we will be **free** one day.

This will be the day—this will be the day when all **God's** children will be able to sing with new meaning, "My country 'tis of thee, sweet land of liberty, of thee I sing. Land where my fathers died, land of the pilgrim's pride. From every mountainside, **let freedom ring."** And if America is to be a great nation, this must become true.

So **let freedom ring** from the prodigious hilltops of New Hampshire. Let **freedom ring** from the mighty mountains of New York. **Let freedom ring** from the heightening Alleghenies of Pennsylvania!

Let freedom ring from the snowcapped Rockies of Colorado! **Let freedom ring** from the curvaceous slopes of California!

But not only that. **Let freedom ring** from Stone Mountain of Georgia!

Let freedom ring from Lookout Mountain of Tennessee!

Let freedom ring from every hill and molehill of Mississippi. From every mountainside, **let freedom ring.**

And when this happens, when we allow **freedom to ring**—when we let it **ring** from every village and every hamlet, from every state and every city—we will be able to speed up that day when all of **God's children,** black men and white men, Jews and Gentiles, Protestants and Catholics, will be able to join hands and sing in the words of the old **Negro** spiritual, **"Free at last! Free at last!** Thank God almighty, we are **free at last!"**

It is important to realize that in order for repetition to be effective, it must be carefully planned, strategically placed, and hardly noticed. That is, repetition can help create an impact on the listener, but it must not call attention to itself. Its purpose is to reinforce the content of a message. Additionally, this speech is not an information speech and does not have the traditionally stated thesis. The message comes in the form of a speech to evoke and repeats the main idea of freedom over and over. As can be seen from his famous speech above and especially from a tape of his speech, Martin Luther King, Jr., was a master in the use of repetition to emphasize his message. He carefully analyzed his occasion, audience, and purpose, creating and delivering one of the most powerful speeches of the century.

Details Provide Support and Proof for the Thesis

Now that you know the thesis for your speech, you know which main ideas you need to support in the body. Rather than wasting time taking extensive notes when you first reviewed each article, book, or documentary, you can now discard material that doesn't relate to your thesis subdivisions and return to only the ones that explain and support these main ideas, taking notes as needed. Remember to write down the magazine, book, or documentary title; the year of publication; and the author's name and title. You need to give credit to any ideas not yours. Citing experts also adds to your support by making you credible because you have obviously done your research and are knowledgeable about your topic.

Supporting details can also come from your own experiences and understanding. If you know how to do something and are showing the techniques involved, you are knowledgeable from your own experience. So briefly tell the audience how you learned it, how long you've been doing it, and then go ahead and demonstrate. If you can also show a couple of books, magazines, or brochures on the subject matter, it helps lend believability to your expertise.

If you are not visually demonstrating something, though, you still need to have details of interest for your audience. One common problem for beginning speakers is the confusion between generalizations and details. Some speakers make the error of restating the same generalization over and over, using slightly different wording each time, rather than using details that support, explain, and prove the general subdivision or main idea. The purpose of the body is to get specific. Listeners enjoy most hearing detailed stories of others in action, whether the stories are humorous anecdotes or serious incidents. But keep in mind, these stories must be directly related to the particular thesis subdivision you are supporting.

Generalizations Without Specifics Are Boring

Let's look at an example using all generalizations as support for the body. The third subdivision from Thesis #4 follows:

Stress affects the body. If you worry about your health, you will find that your body is affected. This worry causes some to feel tired all the time. To rid yourself of this physical effect, you should see a doctor. Also, your body is affected by apprehension in your life. You might be worrying about that job interview or about a test. Other common stresses are caused by problems on the job or in a personal relationship. Some indications are that enough stress can cause ulcers and high blood pressure. So it is easy to see that stress has an affect on the body.

The first attempt at support in this paragraph is that worry causes some to feel tired. But where is an example of someone feeling tired as a result of stress? Where is an expert cited? In this case, an expert would be a medical doctor, a research study, or a case study from a reputable magazine. The next statement is merely repeating that stress exists in a job interview and in school; there is no indication of how such stress affects the body. Where is proof for these assertions? Without supporting details, the generalizations can easily be challenged by listeners. The same is true of the next sentence. The second mention of how the body is affected is in high blood pressure and ulcers. But where are the citations from interviews, TV documentaries, library articles, or books? And where is a sample case study of an actual person who has endured stress and then felt the negative impact on the body? There is no valid supporting detail anywhere in the subdivision.

Using Details Makes a Subdivision Interesting and Memorable

Now let's look at an example using specific details as support for the body. Again the third subdivision from Thesis #4 follows:

Stress affects the body. Dramatic proof of how drastic these effects can be is illustrated by Dr. Bernard Lown, cardiologist from Harvard University. In the introduction to Norman Cousins's book *The Healing Heart*, Dr. Lown tells of a middle-aged librarian who came in for her regular checkup to make sure the digitalis she was taking for her heart was the right amount. Her regular doctor, S. A. Levine, checked her and announced to visiting interns that she had TS. Then he left. Shortly after he was out the door, though, the patient became noticeably upset. So Dr. Lown, who was still in the room, checked her pulse and found it had shot up to 150 a minute. He reexamined her lungs, which had a few minutes before been clear, but now they showed evidence of congestion. When he asked the reason for her sudden nervousness, she said that she knew that the TS meant "terminal situation." Dr. Levine assured her the initials actually meant "tricuspid stenosis." But nothing he said removed her apprehension. He paged her regular doctor, but Dr. Levine could not be located. Shortly thereafter the patient suffered massive pulmonary edema, and later she died from intractable heart failure. Dr. Lown said he never forgot this tragic example of what stress can do to the body.[1] Though this example seems like an unusual extreme, famous surgeon Bernie Siegel's book *Love, Medicine and Miracles* proves it is not. Dr. Siegel cites research about "psychosocial dwarfism," in which a child's growth is severely stunted as a result of an unhealthy emotional atmosphere at home. Research shows that the stress of hostility and rejection in the child's family acts on the hypothalamus gland and stops the production of the needed growth hormone.[2] In another study, Dr. Herbert Benson of Harvard Medical School and author of *The Relaxation Response,* has shown that the body's ability to maintain a healthy cholesterol level is directly related to a person's ability to handle stress.[3] One of the most revealing studies on the effects of stress occurred in 1981. Researcher Madelon Visintainer and two co-workers injected rats with live tumor cells, then regularly subjected them to electric shock. The most stressed group could not evade the shock; the other group was forewarned by a signal and could escape over a barrier. Of the helpless rats, 73 percent contracted cancer; of the less stressed group, only 37 percent got the disease.[4] You and I need to take notice of the negative effects of stress. Even something as usual as exams is stressful enough to harm our bodies. Exam week is when students are more likely to catch colds. According to Dr. Joan Borysenko, the stress of examination periods reduces the level of a particular antibody usually present in saliva, an antibody known to ward off colds. Studies at Ohio State Medical School showed that exam stress also decreased the function of an important lymphocyte called the natural killer cell, which is responsible for patrolling the body and destroying virus-infected cells as well as cancer cells.[5] The overwhelming conclusion of numerous studies is that when we have stress, our bodies often pay a high price.

The above is packed with details, quite different from the generalizations of the first example. After reading the details in the second version, there is no doubt that mental stress can cause bodily harm. Notice how the speaker leads into the details by citing the source of the information. Whenever using anyone's name, include his or her title to prove you are citing people who are experts on your particular topic. These citations add credibility and interest to you as a speaker.

Every subdivision of the thesis needs this type of supporting detail in the body of the speech. The purpose of these specifics is to provide understanding and proof of the main idea, promote interest in the topic, and aid retention of the thesis.

Let's review the supporting detail about stress and notice that before or after each example, the speaker uses the technique of repetition to remind the audience of the topic idea. For example, after the example of the librarian dying because she misinterpreted what TS meant, the speaker says, "Dr. Lown said he never forgot this tragic example of what **stress** can do to the **body**." Notice that the next example about dwarfism again mentions the topic: "Research shows that the **stress** of hostility and rejection. . . ." It would have been just as easy to eliminate the words "the stress of," but by using it the speaker takes advantage of repetition as a memory device and as a transitional bridge. In the next example, both the words **stress** and **body** are used again. And then leading into the detail of the rat experiment, the listener is told, "One of the most effective studies on the effect of **stress** occurred in 1981." The speaker could have jumped right into the example, but then an opportunity for repeating the topic idea of stress would have been lost. And had the speaker not repeated key ideas before an example, the move from one example to the next would be too abrupt.

In fact, there are special tools to use that solve a speaker's problem of abruptness or choppiness. Speakers need to be aware of how to fit ideas smoothly together by using *transitions*—the next step in creating an effective speech.

Notes

1. Norman Cousins, *The Healing Heart*, Avon Books, New York, 1983, pp. 13-14.

2. Bernie S. Siegel, M.D., *Love, Medicine & Miracles*, First Perennial Library edition, New York, 1988, p. 67.

3. Herbert Benson, *The Relaxation Response*, Avon Books, New York, 1976, pp. 46-47.

4. Bernie S. Siegel, M.D., *Love, Medicine & Miracles*, Harper & Row, New York, 1986, pp. 72-73.

5. Joan Borysenko, *Minding the Body, Mending the Mind*, Addison-Wesley, New York, 1987, p. 16.

8 Using Transitions

Earlier you learned that the use of repetition helps a person retain information. Furthermore, without the repetition and the use of transitions, the audience tends to forget which subdivision of the thesis you are proving, which is the reason for having the detail in the first place. Let's look at transitions in more detail.

Transitions Link Ideas and Offer a Chance for Repetition

The word *transition* means "to move across or through"; the meaning comes from the first part of the word *trans,* which means "across." The meaning is easy to understand when you consider that *transportation* moves us "across" town, "across" states, "across" the nation, or "across" the world. When we go through *transitions* in life, we "move across" or "through" stages of time and experience.

Transitions are frequently called signposts because they help alert your listener to where you are in your speech. Like road signs guiding travelers by informing them how far is left to go and what town is being entered, signposts guide listeners by informing them how far the speaker is in the speech and what thesis subdivision is being supported.

Transitions in the language help a speaker (or writer) move smoothly across examples or across main ideas. There are two types of transitions.

Using Transitional Words or Phrases

Transitional words or phrases are short, consisting of either a single word or a two-, three-, or four-word phrase. Below is a listing of transitional words and short phrases that help movement of ideas flow smoothly. You will want to use them in your speeches.

TRANSITIONAL WORDS AND PHRASES

These signals make your movement of ideas and examples clear to your listener. To move from one subdivision to another or one example to another, choose from the following list.

Accordingly
Also
As a result
As I have said
As a result
As has been noted
Besides
Clearly then
Consequently
Equally important
Eventually
Finally
First, second, third
For example
For instance
Furthermore
Hence
Immediately
In addition
In brief

In conclusion (*When speaking, this phrase is used only in the actual conclusion of the whole speech; it is not used anywhere else*)
In other words
In short
In the same way
In sum
Later
Likewise
Meanwhile
Moreover
Next
Of course
Similarly
So
Subsequently
Then
Therefore
Thus
To begin with
To sum up

To show a contrast or introduce another point of view, choose from the following.

After all	On the contrary
But	On the other hand
Conversely	Otherwise
However	Still
In contrast	Yet
Nevertheless	

As the speaker, you know exactly where you are going, but your audience does not possess that same knowledge. Therefore, you need to prepare the listeners by sending them verbal signals. These signals are transitions or signposts.

DO-IT EXERCISE

Pick out the transitional words or phrases from the following paragraph:

Beginning speakers often must cope with the feeling of nervousness. To begin with, they find the tension so uncomfortable that they would rather not learn to speak in public at all. Furthermore, when a beginner actually experiences standing in front of a group for the first time, he or she may feel the face flush, the hands sweat, and the legs shake. In addition, when the speech begins, the voice may quiver, and the mouth often feels like it has cotton in it. Meanwhile, the speaker is supposed to be concentrating on delivering a speech—a tough task indeed!

ANSWERS TO "DO-IT EXERCISE"

The standard short transitions in the previous paragraph are as follows:

1. To begin with
2. Furthermore
3. In addition
4. Meanwhile

Using the Transitional Hook

Think of the transitional hook in terms of a fish hook. It reaches back to the wording or the ideas in a previous sentence and repeats or restates that wording while moving into a new idea or example. Transitions are used out of consideration for your listener and as an effective tool for repetition.

DO-IT EXERCISE

Pick out the transitional hooks from the following paragraph:

Beginning speakers often must cope with the feeling of nervousness. This nervousness can be so uncomfortable that the beginner would rather not learn to speak in public at all. The desire to avoid getting in front of a group results from what frequently happens with the very first experience. The beginner may feel the face flush, the hands sweat, and the legs shake. As if these embarrassments aren't enough, when the beginner starts to talk, he or she may have a quivery voice and a mouth that feels like cotton is in it. During all these negative reactions, the speaker is supposed to be concentrating on delivering a speech—a tough task indeed!

ANSWERS TO "DO-IT EXERCISE"

The transitional hooks in the previous paragraph are as follows:

1. This nervousness
2. The desire to avoid getting in front ...
3. As if these embarrassments
4. During all these negative reactions

The hook is considered a stronger transition than the standard transitional word or phrase because the hook allows for a restatement of key ideas. Thus the hook serves not only as a smooth way to move from one idea to another but also as a valuable memory technique.

Using Both Types of Transitions Within a Subdivision

Now let's look again at the sample subdivision on stress that was presented in Chapter 7 on "Supporting Your Thesis." Transitional words or phrases are in italics, and transitional hooks are in boldface type.

Stress affects the body. Dramatic proof of how drastic **these effects** can be is illustrated by Dr. Bernard Lown, cardiologist from Harvard University. In the introduction to the Norman Cousins book *The Healing Heart,* Dr. Lown tells of a middle-aged librarian who came in for her regular check-up to make sure the digitalis she was taking for her heart was the right amount. Her regular doctor, S. A. Levine, checked her and announced to visiting interns that she had TS. *Then* he left. *Shortly after* he was out the door, *though,* the patient became noticeably upset. *So* Dr. Lown, who was still in the room, checked her pulse and found it had shot up to 150 a minute. He reexamined her lungs, which had a few minutes before been clear, but now they showed evidence of congestion. When he asked the reason for her sudden nervousness, she said that she knew that the TS meant "terminal situation." Dr. Levine assured her the initials actually meant "tricuspid stenosis." *But* nothing he said removed her apprehension. He paged her regular doctor, *but* Dr. Levine could not be located. Shortly *thereafter* the patient suffered massive pulmonary edema, and *later* she died from intractable heart failure. Dr. Lown said he never forgot **this tragic example** of what **stress** can do to the body.[1] *Though* **this example** seems like an unusual extreme, famous surgeon Bernie Siegel's book *Love, Medicine and Miracles,* proves it is not. Dr. Siegel cites **research** about "psychosocial dwarfism," in which a child's growth is severely stunted as a result of an unhealthy emotional atmosphere at home. Research shows that the **stress** of hostility and rejection in the child's family acts on the hypothalamus gland and stops the production of the needed growth hormone.[2] In *another* study, Dr. Herbert Benson of Harvard Medical School and author of *The Relaxation Response,* has shown that the body's ability to maintain a healthy cholesterol level is directly related to a person's ability to handle **stress.**[3] *One* of the most revealing **studies** on the effects of **stress** occurred in 1981. Researcher Madelon Visintainer and two co-workers injected rats with live tumor cells, *then* regularly subjected them to electric shock. The most **stressed** group could not evade the shock; the other group was forewarned by a signal and could escape over a barrier. Of the helpless rats, 73 percent contracted cancer; of the less **stressed** group, only 37 percent got the disease.[4] You and I need to take notice of the negative effects of **stress**. *Even* something as usual as **exams** is **stressful** enough to harm our bodies. **Exam** week is when students are more likely to catch colds. According to Dr. Joan Borysenko, the **stress** of **examination** periods reduces the level of a particular antibody usually present in saliva, an antibody known to ward off colds. **Studies** at Ohio State Medical School showed that exam **stress** *also* decreased the function of an important lymphocyte known as the natural killer cell, which is responsible for patrolling the body and destroying virus-infected cells as well as cancer cells.[5] **The overwhelming conclusion of numerous studies is that when we have stress, our bodies often pay a high price.**

In this detailed subdivision on stress, the words *shortly after, though, even, one, then, so, but, thereafter, later, another,* and *also* are single word transitions.

Many of the transitions, however, are transitional hooks, for they restate or repeat the main idea (as shown in the last chapter), hence smoothly reminding the listener of the topic while, at the same time, working as a memory device.

The final sentence of the subdivision reminds the audience of the first sentence generalization and is itself a generalization. This transitional sentence at the end of the subdivision lets the audience know that the speaker has finished all examples for this area and will be moving into a new broad category of the body, which will have its own supporting examples. This last transitional sentence is mandatory and is not created for the speaker, but rather it is solely to move the listener smoothly out of one subdivision and into the next.

Perhaps now you understand why transitional words and phrases as well as transitional hooks are important tools for the speaker. Both types of transitions or signposts are necessary to help the listener follow the organization and should be interspersed throughout your speech.

Using Transitions Throughout Your Entire Speech

Let's suppose that a speaker is to present a self-introduction speech to an audience. The goal is to get the speaker to experience getting in front of a group and to get the group to know the speaker as a personality, not just a strange face. Below is a sample speech **without transitions.**

> You and I have a lot in common. We are after a degree in our chosen major. You think your major will ultimately make you happy. I hope you are right. I am more fortunate than some of you. I do not just *THINK* my major will make me happy; I *KNOW*. It already has. The reason I know is because of my experiences. You will be able to remember me because of my name, my employer, and my interests and how they are all interconnected.
>
> My name is easy to remember. My name came about because my parents (like some of yours) named me after another relative—my grandfather. They wanted one that was simple. I think that resulted from the fact that my father's first and middle name is Maurice Maynard. That isn't an easy name. People misspell it. They write it "Morris." Dad simplifies matters and goes by the nickname Mac. My mother's first and middle name is Hattie Marie. She has always gone by the name Pat. My name is Sammy Sams. The correct name is Samuel Sams (after my mother's father). I was christened with the shortened form Sammy Sams. Some people tell me it sounds like a stage name.
>
> I am employed part time. I am employed at Good Samaritan Hospital. Sammy Sams works at Good Sam. I am an assistant in the physical therapy department. I help others rehabilitate their muscles and gain full use of their limbs. My job makes me happy. I watch someone who has been injured set aside crutches and take the first small steps to recuperation. I watch a victim of an accident overcome inability to use an arm or hand. I have seen smiles appear on faces that moments before revealed pain; I have seen tears of happiness replace tears of sadness; I have witnessed success by someone using a limb after she had been told she would never be able to use it again!
>
> I give some of my time as a volunteer to an organization called Riding For The Handicapped. It offers physically or mentally handicapped children and adults the chance to increase their abilities by experiencing horseback riding. The theory is that sometimes when traditional rehabilitation therapy fails, a nontraditional one may not. Participation in sports is assumed to be impossible for someone with extreme physical or mental limitations; teachers in this program believe that the excitement of petting a horse and of feeling a horse's muscles working beneath a handicapped rider whose muscles do not work so well will be beneficial. It will excite the rider when the realization "hits" that he or she will be riding a horse regularly. Actually riding the horse allows the rider to feel the horse's muscles at work.

I have experienced wonderful success stories. I watched as a rider could not sit on the horse without being held on by the two spotters; one person on the left of the saddle and one on the right are always available to catch or support a rider. Joe had been riding for eight weeks and had to be held up by the two spotters; I was one. During the ninth week, Joe seemed to be riding rather well. The teachers motioned me and the other spotter to let go of him. We cautiously did, and there was Joe sitting in the saddle and riding a horse without any help. I'll never forget Joe's laugh when he realized what had happened, and I'll never forget the tears in his mother's eyes as she watched a miracle occur.

I am helping ordinary people in real-life scenes, and I am watching them turn real-life handicaps and tragedies into heroic accomplishments and real-life miracles.

Now let's look at the same speech *with transitions.* Both transitional words and phrases and transitional hooks (repetitions) are highlighted.

You and I have a lot in common. We are after **the same basic goal,** a degree in our chosen major. You think your major will ultimately make you happy. I hope you are right, **but** I am more fortunate than some of you *because* I do not just *THINK* my major will make me happy; I *KNOW* **because** it already has **brought me much happiness.** The reason I know **that I will be happy with my major** is because of my experiences **that I am about to share with you.** You will be able to remember me because of my name, my employer, and my interests and how they are all interconnected.

First, my name **is one that** is easy to remember **because the first and last are alike.** My name came about because my parents (like some of yours) named me after another relative—**in this case,** my grandfather. **But** they **also** wanted one that was simple. I think that resulted from the fact that my father's first and middle name is Maurice Maynard. **Not only isn't that an easy name but also people hear the first name and write it incorrectly.** They write it "Morris" **as in the famous television cat, Morris.** So Dad simplifies matters and goes by the nickname Mac. **Similar to my father's difficult name,** my mother's first and middle names are Hattie Marie; **she so much hates her name that almost no one knows her real name because** she has always gone by the name Pat. **And, no, I have no idea how she got the name Pat out of Hattie Marie. Well, so far, you know my name is not going to be Maurice or Maynard, and it certainly isn't Hattie or Marie.** My name **(first and last)** is Sammy Sams. **Simple, isn't it? Actually,** the correct name is Samuel Sams (after my mother's father), but **even as a child,** I was christened with the shortened form Sammy Sams. Some people tell me it sounds like a stage name. **Even so, acting is not what Sammy Sams is interested in doing with his life.**

What I am interested in doing with my life, I am already doing where I am employed part-time. My employer not only makes me happy but also serves as a way for you to remember my name. Oddly enough I am employed at Good Samaritan Hospital. **Yes,** Sammy Sams works at Good Sam. **As humorous as this may sound to you (and I admit it is unusual), I am very serious about my employment** as an assistant in the physical therapy department. **This work I do to** help others rehabilitate their muscles and gain full use of their limbs makes me happy. **I gain fulfillment when** I watch someone who has been injured set aside crutches and take the first small steps to recuperation. **I feel happy inside when** I watch a victim of an accident overcome inability to use an arm or hand. I have seen smiles appear on faces that moments before revealed pain; I have seen tears of happiness replace tears of sadness; I have witnessed success by someone using a limb after she had been told she would never be able to use it again! **Yes, my job at Good Sam brings me great joy, and I am here at this college to gain more training in physical therapy because I know it will help me gain ground on my road to happiness.**

Now you know that Sammy Sams works at Good Sam, but you do not know my interests outside of my job. Though I have many, I am going to share with you just one—one that is interconnected to my job. One of my outside interests is giving my time as a volunteer to an organization called Riding For The Handicapped. **This organization** offers physically or mentally handicapped children and adults the chance to increase their abilities by experiencing horseback riding. The theory **behind Riding For The Handicapped** is that sometimes when traditional rehabilitation therapy **(such as that in a hospital)** fails, a nontraditional one may not. **Frequently,** participation in sports is assumed to be impossible for someone with extreme physical or mental limitations; **however,** teachers in this program believe that the excitement of petting a horse and of feeling a horse's muscles working beneath a handicapped rider whose muscles do not work so well will **do two things: one,** it will excite the rider when the realization "hits" that he or she will be riding a horse regularly, **and two,** actually riding the horse allows the rider to feel the horse's muscles at work. **As with my job in physical therapy,** I have experienced wonderful success stories. **Once** I watched as a rider could not sit on the horse without being held on by the two spotters; **that is,** one person on the left of the saddle and one on the right are always available to catch or support a rider. **This particular rider,** Joe, had been riding for eight weeks and had to be held up by the two spotters; I was **one of those spotters.** During the ninth week, Joe seemed to be riding rather well,

and the teachers motioned me and the other spotter to let go of him. We cautiously did, and there was Joe sitting in the saddle and riding a horse without any help. I'll never forget Joe's laugh when he realized what had happened, and I'll never forget the tears in his mother's eyes as she watched a miracle occur. **My combining traditional physical therapy at a hospital with nontraditional therapy as a volunteer for Riding For The Handicapped allows me options about how to best help people overcome their limitations.**

Sammy Sams may sound like a stage name, but my job at Good Sam and my volunteering for Riding For The Handicapped are more exciting to me than acting. Rather than performing a make-believe scene with make-believe heroes, I am helping ordinary people in real-life scenes, and I am watching them turn real-life handicaps and tragedies into heroic accomplishments and real-life miracles.

Transitions exist within the introduction (the first paragraph), the body (the three middle paragraphs), and the conclusion (the last paragraph). They are also used when moving from the introduction to the body, when moving from one subdivision in the body to another subdivision in the body, and when moving from the last subdivision of the body to the conclusion. Any movement needs to be smooth to the listener; transitions fulfill this need.

The introduction of a speech not only serves as a transition into the body but also fulfills additional functions. Since each speech needs an introduction before the body, a beginning speaker needs to learn how to create an introduction so that it fulfills its purposes, while moving smoothly into the body. The next chapter explains how to create both introductions and conclusions, your next step in speech preparation.

Notes

1. Norman Cousins, *The Healing Heart*, Avon Books, New York, 1983, pp. 13-14.

2. Bernie S. Siegel, M.D., *Love, Medicine & Miracles*, First Perennial Library edition, New York, 1988, p. 67.

3. Herbert Benson, *The Relaxation Response*, Avon Books, New York, 1976, pp. 46-47.

4. Bernie S. Siegel, M.D., *Love, Medicine & Miracles*, Harper & Row, New York, 1986, pp. 72-73.

5. Joan Borysenko, *Minding the Body, Mending the Mind*, Addison-Wesley, New York, 1987, p. 16.

9 Creating Your Introduction and Conclusion

When you create the introduction and conclusion of a speech, you have already performed several necessary steps of speech preparation: You have analyzed the audience, chosen the topic, researched in the library, organized a thesis statement, and supported each subdivision of the thesis. Now that you have the body of the speech created, you know lots of interesting facts about your topic. This knowledge, along with a little creative thinking, affords you enough to prepare both the introduction and conclusion. First, let's look at the introduction. In order to have a good introduction, you need to know why it exists.

The Introduction Serves at Least Three Purposes

The introduction to a speech provides benefits to both the speaker and the listener. All introductions should fulfill at least the following three purposes:

1. Gain audience attention
2. Establish relevance for the audience
3. Tell the organization for the speech in a thesis statement

Let's look at each purpose more closely.

The most important moment for the speaker is the first impression. First impressions occur the moment the audience first sees and hears the speaker. These precious beginning seconds and minutes should be planned carefully to make the best impression possible.

Many times I have seen a speaker appear uncomfortable at the beginning of a speech because the introduction was not planned. In this situation the speaker either jumps right into the body of the speech without giving any forewarning or fumbles around with awkward wording until he or she can clumsily work out of the introduction into the body. Either way establishes a negative impression and causes the audience to question the speaker's ability and credibility.

"Grab" the Attention of the Audience

Before an audience will listen to you, you have to get their attention; hence, the attention-getter is the first function of the introduction. Fulfilling this function requires both patience and creativity. The patience is needed when a speaker first walks to the lectern. If members of the audience are talking, reading, or otherwise occupied, the speaker must stand in silence until people begin to realize someone is in front of them. If you learn to have some patience, you will see the power of silence: People will begin hushing one another until all are silent and full attention is directed toward you. These riveted stares can be unnerving if you are a beginning speaker, but this is the moment when you hold the most power. How successful you are in keeping their attention as you say your first words depends on your creativity. If you have something that jolts the audience, they will continue to listen. If you begin by faltering for words, you will in effect tell the audience you are not prepared and that you did not care enough about them to put forth effort for them, and so you will lose the listeners' attention. If you start by sounding bored, you will also lose their attention. Your insurance against losing your audience in the beginning of your speech is to create an attention-grabber.

You must think of some clever way to begin the speech. You might tell a story, cite an anecdote, or use a catchy phrase. You can use a prop, show a visual aid, act out something, or involve the audience.

For example, years ago one of my students was giving a speech on exercising that business professionals can do while stuck in their offices and in their business attire. When his name was called to speak, he walked to the desk and stood behind the lectern. He was appropriately wearing a business suit, white shirt, and tie. He paused initially until he had the audience silent and looking at him.

Then he told the audience that he knew most of them were planning to enter the business world where they would dress in suits and sit at a desk all day. He further informed them that the term *middle-age spread* had come about because of a truth: As people age, the gaining of weight becomes more and more of a problem, increasing health risks, lowering self-esteem, and raising clothing costs. The simple solution, the student continued, was in a program of exercise. As he said this, he walked around the desk so the audience could see him, and he quickly took off his tie and placed it on an empty chair. Now as he talked, he began unbuttoning his shirt. He had all eyes riveted to him; audience attention was running at 100 percent. He told of the need for an outfit to sweat in, and then he took off his suit jacket and, with his shirt unbuttoned, he began undoing his belt.

Now, a couple of the listeners looked at me to see if I was going to stop the stripping act, but I ignored them as he had already okayed his plan with me. They quickly turned their attention back to the speaker because they didn't want to miss anything. The audience laughed as he quickly pulled off his pants to show tights underneath and said "Fooled you." Then he walked behind the lectern again and told them that this double layer of attire would be ridiculous in an office atmosphere. But, he told them he had a new solution for them—a new kind of exercise that could be executed in a suit, without wearing any exercise outfit underneath, without using any exercise equipment, and within the confines of an office. He proceeded to discuss three aspects of isometric exercises, and he got the class involved in doing some of them.

This student's creativity helped him fulfill the first obligation of any speaker: grabbing the attention of the audience. Note how his introduction related to the content of his speech.

Not only can you do something that gets the attention of the audience, but you can also word your speech in such a way that you create surprise or intrigue. Below are two examples. The first is an introduction that is unplanned and weak because it has no attention-getter and no thesis. In fact, it rambles around and confuses the audience members—whether or not they know the game being discussed. The second example is on the same topic but has an attention-getter and a thesis.

INTRODUCTION NOT FULFILLING MAJOR PURPOSES

Lots of people like sports, and I like one too. It gives me enjoyment, and I plan to participate again soon. You've got to be careful, and when you get shot with the gun, don't think it doesn't hurt. It really stings, and then you're out of the game. You can play it indoors at some special places, but I like to play out-of-doors in a woods.

INTRODUCTION FULFILLING MAJOR PURPOSES

In 1992, I was in a woods in Kentucky and was shot.

As if this occurrence weren't frustrating enough for me, I was again shot a few months later under much the same circumstances. As you can see, I survived. I'm here to tell you how you, too, can survive being shot—and even enjoy it! The enjoyment comes from a new game or sport. Paintball is the name of this adult-type game, and you are about to learn about the rules, equipment, location, and cost.

The difference between the above introductions is striking. The first in no way works to grab the audience's attention and make them eager to hear what follows. The second does.

Another way to gain audience attention and interest is to cite some true story relating to the topic. These stories, anecdotes, or case studies will come from your reading of articles, books, newspapers. They might come from watching news programs or documentaries or from listening to the radio. Once you know your topic, you want to keep alert for any material that might have potential for gaining audience attention. For example, below are two introductions. The first is weak in the area of gaining attention; it just jumps right into the topic. The second is stronger because it gains attention and interests the audience before they know what the topic is.

INTRODUCTION WITHOUT ATTENTION-GETTER

Waste disposal is a problem for Americans. We need to be conscious that dumping garbage is costly for our health and for our pocketbooks.

INTRODUCTION WITH ATTENTION-GETTER

As a cold rain drizzles onto her beat-up Pontiac parked beside a country road, Terri Moore watches and waits. She is on **"dump patrol."** Suddenly an 18-wheeler rounds the bend. Mrs. Moore jumps from the car, peers through her binoculars, and barks into a tape recorder, "New Jersey truck plate. More trash from the East." The truck is headed to the Center Point Indiana Sanitary Landfill. Just a few years ago, only about two trucks a day would dump trash at this facility, and it was all local trash. Now, not just 2 but rather 20 to 30 semitrailers roll into this little town of 250 people every day, dumping garbage—and most aren't from Indiana, let alone Center Point. In the first three months of this year, about 75% of the trash coming into Center Point came from New York, New Jersey, and Philadelphia (April 26, 1991, *The Wall Street Journal*). This account introduces a nationwide problem that affects you and me—a problem that jeopardizes our health and costs us money.

The second introduction above tells a story that leads people into the topic in an intriguing way. It makes them curious enough to keep listening, and that is the goal of an attention-getter.

It is possible, however, to have an attention-getter that goes beyond the boundary of acceptance or good taste.

"Don'ts" of a Speech Introduction

For example, many years ago I had a student who walked up to the front of the class to give his speech. He had carried something in a sack to the desk and proceeded to take out a glass. Then he walked over to one side of the room, drew back the hand holding the glass, and threw it with all his might into the corner of the room. The glass shattered into thousands of tiny pieces. The audience (including me) was so astonished that they at first stared in disbelief, then looked at each other, and then laughed in amazement. Some began talking with one another and wouldn't be quiet. So he had to begin his speech with audience members whispering to one another about what had just happened. He had breached the first three of the following important "don'ts" of a speech introduction:

1. Don't endanger an audience. (Shattering glass is dangerous.)
2. Don't make a speech introduction so intense that it overpowers the rest of what you say. (The goal is to get the audience to listen **to what follows** the introduction.)
3. Don't use introductory content that is not related to your speech topic. (His attention grabber had no relationship to the content of his speech.)
4. Don't use any material that might offend any member of the audience. If you think a joke you'd like to tell might insult even one person, don't use it. If you have a short anecdote that might be taken in a negative way, avoid telling it. I tell speakers to remember the following simple rule: WHEN IN DOUBT, DON'T.
5. Don't let the first words out of your mouth be "Today, I'm going to tell you . . ." or some such similar statement. We've already established that your first words should be something that grabs audience attention and is unique to your topic. The words above are so general that every speaker in the world could use them for any topic; hence, such a beginning has no uniqueness or interest factor.
6. Don't assume your audience will laugh at what you think is funny. If you have a sense of humor and feel at ease using it in a speech, keep in mind that not everyone thinks the same thing is funny. So if you use humor, plan it as if you do not expect the audience to laugh. That way,

if you do not get laughter, you are prepared and can continue your speech; if you do get the laughter, it becomes a bonus.

Establish Relevance for the Audience

The second major role of a speech introduction is to relate to the lives of the audience. That is, either you must show the audience the information will be valuable in their lives, or else the topic must be so unique that the audience is automatically interested.

For example, let's say our topic is cancer. Most people know that there are a variety of cancers, and many do not see this topic as unique because it is constantly in front of us via newspapers, magazines, radio, and TV. So something has to be done to create interest anew and to show the topic is relevant to the lives of the audience. Telling about someone getting cancer and merely announcing symptoms isn't enough.

Though there are a variety of good ways that relevance and interest could be achieved, the following illustrates but one of them.

The speaker approaches the front of the audience with two large and three small posters in hand. The audience cannot see any of them as they are all placed face down on the desk. The speaker looks at the audience and lifts the first large poster for all to see. Reaction is quick, as some of the males whistle under their breath and make brief comments like, "This is more like it," "Give me an address," and "Let's see another."

Some members chuckle; the audience is viewing a huge picture of a very curvaceous woman, clad in a bikini and evenly tanned, leaning against a surfboard on a beachfront. As the poster is put away, the speaker says, "I believe in equal time" and then lifts a second large poster so the audience can see. This time, a female says, "All right!" and everybody laughs. The picture on this poster is a very tan and muscular male in tight swim trunks.

Then the speaker lays the poster back down and, looking at the audience, says, "These pictures **seem** to indicate two very attractive and very healthy people—people we envy just by looking at their well-built, tanned bodies—people we would like to look like. But now I would like you to look at another picture." The speaker now holds up another poster, this one with a picture of a grotesque-looking sore on someone's arm, and says, "Who would guess that such healthy-looking bodies as you just saw have something about them that is not healthy. Who would guess that in our attempts this spring and summer to gain the healthy glow of a golden tan, we might end up looking like this (points directly to horrible wound in the picture)? Do you know what a tan really is? It is the skin's protective action against the rays of the sun, our bodies' natural defense against danger." The student puts down the poster and looks at the audience, saying, "I know that many of us believe that we needn't worry about skin cancer, and I know we will go bask in the sun this summer just as we planned. But if statistics from a 1988 brochure of the National Cancer Institute fit this room, 40 to 50 percent of us will be the victim of skin cancer sometime in our lives. Which half of this audience will it be?" Then he pointed to two rows and said, "Will it be these two rows? Or maybe these two?"

Now the speaker reaches for another poster, and before turning it around so the audience can see, says, "And if the some of us who get skin cancer do not discover it soon enough, we will also be another kind of victim." When the poster is turned around, the audience sees a closed coffin surrounded by flowers in a funeral home setting. The speaker says, "Death's victim."

So far, the speaker has grabbed attention by using the first two posters. He also created interest and relevance by showing the audience additional pictures (of a shocking nature contrasted with the first two), by relating to the typical experiences of the audience, and by telling the audience that several of them will likely have skin cancer sometime in their lives. This topic now relates to the lives of this audience and fulfills the second function of the introduction: establishment of relevance.

Now, the third purpose of the speech introduction is all that remains to be accomplished.

State the Organization of the Speech in a Thesis

Chapter 6 details how to develop a good thesis statement. What is important here is that you realize the thesis is first announced in the introduction of your speech, is placed at the end of that introduction, and is formed into a single sentence containing items in a series; each element of the series is one of the subdivisions in the body. Hence, by the time your introduction to your speech is done, the audience knows how many points you will support in the body of the speech. Immediately after the thesis, the speaker moves into only the first subdivision, which begins the first section of the body of the speech.

In the case of the speech on skin cancer used above, the speaker ended the introduction using the following thesis: Avoid the serious consequences of major surgery or death by learning the **SKIN** of skin cancer; that is, (1) skimming your skin, (2) knowing the danger signals, (3) investigating current treatments, and (4) noting available specialists.

At this point, the introduction is finished and has fulfilled all its obligations to the audience. If you will recall, those obligations were three in number. To make it easy for you to remember them, putting together the first letter of each requirement spells the word **GET** (as in how a speaker is supposed to **get** smoothly and interestingly into the body of the speech); in summary, they are (1) **grab** the attention of the audience, (2) **explain** relevance to the audience's experience, and (3) **tell** the speech organization in a thesis.

Though the introduction appears to be only for the audience, it is also for the speaker. A good introduction gives the speaker a chance to bond with the audience, to feel in control of the situation, and to build confidence and self-esteem. Furthermore, the thesis forces the speaker to stay on the topic and have a clear sense of direction, which, in turn, benefits the audience.

Also of benefit to the audience is the conclusion. Since you know when you are finished, it would be convenient to merely walk to your chair and sit down after you are finished with the body of the speech. Or it would be easy to conclude by saying, "Okay, that's all folks." Easy—but not powerful. If you can repeat in your mind that the conclusion is FOR THE AUDIENCE, you will better comprehend its value to you as a speaker.

The Conclusion Serves at Least Three Purposes

A conclusion, like the introduction, has three roles to perform:

1. To **e**nd with finality
2. To **n**ame the subdivisions of the thesis
3. To **d**enote power in the last sentence

The first letter of each of these purposes spells **"end"** for the end of the speech.

End Your Speech With Finality

The most logical purpose of a speech conclusion is to make the audience aware that you are done in a smooth way. "Finality" means "the condition of being complete." Thus you are giving a sense of completeness to your audience.

When you are ready to move into the conclusion, you are moving out of the last subdivision of the body of the speech. One way to signal the audience that you are in the conclusion is to make a generalization about the topic of the speech, frequently by referring back to the attention-getter in the introduction. Below are the first sentences of two conclusions. The first one refers to the topic, but it does nothing to tie into the attention-getter. The second one is smoother and hooks back into the attention-getter.

FIRST SENTENCE OF CONCLUSION
WITH REFERENCE ONLY TO BASIC TOPIC

I hope you like paintball as much as I do.

FIRST SENTENCE OF CONCLUSION
WITH REFERENCE TO ATTENTION-GETTER

Now you understand how my getting shot twice in a woods in Kentucky was an experience I willingly paid to have.

The first example above is abrupt and trite. The second is smoother because it serves as a transitional hook back to the most interesting aspect of the introduction.

Some speakers are tempted to use transitional words that announce clearly that they are in the conclusion. Such words as "in conclusion," "in summary," and "finally" will serve the purpose but are not usually considered as strong as the transitional hook.

NOTE: In a speech the words "in conclusion" are used only in the actual speech conclusion. They are never to be used anywhere in the introduction or anywhere in the body. Though this rule is not true in writing, it is always true in speaking. These words in a speech notify the listener that the speech is almost over. But please also note that none of the sample speeches in this text begin with the words "in conclusion." Some believe that this phrase is a weak way to move into a speech conclusion and prefer the use of more content-oriented material, such as the transitional hook provides.

Name the Main Ideas of the Thesis

The speaker should use the opportunity of a speech conclusion to restate all the subdivisions of the thesis. If you will recall, the only other time the subdivisions were mentioned all at one time occurred in the introduction. In the body each subdivision is stated separately and is separately supported with details. So the conclusion affords the speaker the chance to use the memory device of repeating the subdivisions all together.

Furthermore, by returning to the general statements of the thesis and moving away from the specific details mandatory in the body of the speech, the speaker ensures that the audience is aware the end of the speech is near. The restatement of subdivisions usually falls in the middle of the conclusion. In the case of the second example about the sport of paintball above, the thesis restatement would come after the transitional hook and would look similar to the following.

CONCLUSION CONTAINING THESIS RESTATEMENT

Now you understand how my getting shot twice in a woods in Kentucky was an experience I willingly paid to have. You also now know the rules involved, the equipment needed, the places nearby, and the costs incurred to participate in paintball.

Now we have fulfilled the first two functions of a speech conclusion and the remaining one is, perhaps, the hardest to accomplish.

Denote Power in the Last Sentence

The final goal of a speaker is to have a powerful ending. As you walk to your seat, members of the audience should be left thinking about some aspect of your speech. Your speech should have some kind of a punch in the last sentence. Let's continue with the topic of paintball again.

CONCLUSION FULFILLING ALL THREE REQUIREMENTS

Now you understand how my getting shot twice in a woods in Kentucky was an experience I willingly paid to have. You also now know the rules involved, the equipment needed, the places nearby, and the costs incurred to participate in paintball. I am personally inviting any and all of you to a showdown by joining me when I go next Saturday to a shootout you will never forget!

Now let's look at one more conclusion with all three functions fulfilled. This one is on the topic of alcoholism.

CONCLUSION FULFILLING ALL THREE REQUIREMENTS

When I began, I mentioned that some of you may know an alcohol abuser and some may not. Furthermore, I have shown you that understanding the mood swings, drinking signals, and behavior patterns of alcoholics may help you identify the problem in yourself or in a loved one. Now I'd like to inform you that **all** of you do know someone with an alcohol problem; you are looking at her. And my guess is you know more than just one—whether or not you realize it.

Notice that these conclusions are brief and yet fulfill the requirements. The first sentence makes it apparent that the speaker has left the details of the body of the speech and is moving into the conclusion. The next sentence reiterates the thesis, using the speaker's tool of repetition. Then the last sentence is a powerful one that leaves the audience thinking about the topic discussed and makes a memorable impression.

There are numerous ways to end a speech: a reminder of a particularly poignant story told in the body, a personal story that relates to the topic, a humorous incident, a tragic occurrence, a hypothetical situation, and so forth. The important points to remember are that you feel comfortable with your ending, that it relates to your topic, and that you fulfill the three criteria of a conclusion.

Before we leave this important final stage of the content of a speech, I must point out two of the most common problems a speaker will face in creating and delivering a speech conclusion. These problems exist for all levels of speakers: (1) making the conclusion too short and (2) making the conclusion too long.

Do Not Make the Conclusion Too Short

The shortest conclusion is no conclusion at all. I have heard speakers who, when they finished the final subdivision in the body of the speech, abruptly sat down. At this point, the audience members usually look at one another with a questioning look, wondering if the speaker is okay. Since the conclusion is FOR THE AUDIENCE, the audience members, in cases such as these, are shocked that the speaker quit. They are not given that sense of finality and closure they expect, and so the speech content suffers because the audience is not left thinking about the speech, but rather they are thinking about the fact the speaker never finished and wondering if something is wrong.

Let me share a personal story with you that might help you see how natural it is for all of us to expect finality. When I graduated from college and accepted a position at a campus in the Midwest, I moved into an apartment complex where an elderly lady (Vi) befriended me.

When I finally got a phone installed in my apartment, I called Vi to give her my phone number. She was elated that I had a phone, and we chatted awhile. Then suddenly, she was no longer on the line. I called her name, but got no response. It occurred to me she might have had a heart attack, but before dialing an ambulance, I quickly dialed her number. After the first ring, she answered the phone. I said, "Vi, are you all right?" She responded, "What do you mean, 'Am I all right'? Of course I am; you just talked to me!" Relieved and surprised, I replied, "Oh. It was just a funny feeling I had. I'm glad you're okay. Bye."

What I discovered was that whenever Vi was finished talking on the phone, she would hang up. If there was nothing more to say, I guess she figured why waste time. And I learned to accept her unusual phone habit. But I realized then how much all of us rely on conclusions—even with something as simple as a phone call.

If you would like to verify this idea, I suggest you try a little experiment. Next time you are on the phone with a good friend and are done with the conversation, hang up. Wait just a moment, and if the friend doesn't call to check on you, call him or her back so that you still have a friend. The point here is that we always prepare the person on the other end of the line for our ending by saying such things as "Well, I've got to be going," "Someone's at the door," "I have to go now," "Someone's on the other line," "I'll talk to you later," "Take care now," and other such comments. This is all in preparation for that very last line: "Goodbye." We give this forewarning to others, and we expect a conclusion from them in return.

Why, then, should it be hard to understand that we expect this same courtesy, forewarning, and finality from a public speaker?

Do Not Make the Conclusion Too Long

As disconcerting as an abrupt conclusion can be, I think that the worst offense is the overly long conclusion.

Haven't you ever heard a speaker (at a graduation, at a sales presentation, at a political gathering, at a church function) who prepared the listener for the conclusion, but then kept going on and on and on? This is the time when the audience is fidgeting in their seats, looking at their watches, shuffling their feet, clearing their throats, and indicating their impatience. Clearly, they have been betrayed. What has been promised (the conclusion, the finish) is not given.

Again, let me cite an illustration that I am sure all of us have shared.

Let's say that Mary and Joe plan a winter party and invite several couples. The party goes quite well, and all have gone home except for one couple. Finally, one of them says, "Well, we better be going." And they both stand. So Mary and Joe stand also, and Joe goes to get their coats. When he brings them back, both visitors put on their coats but remain in place talking for another fifteen minutes.

It may be at this point, the host and hostess are thinking, "How do we get them to the door?" At the same time, the visitors may be thinking, "How do we gracefully make it to the door?" Finally someone makes a motion, and with relief, all head to the door. Then all four stand at the door for another ten minutes. By the time the couple leaves, sweat is pouring down their backs from having stood inside the house with their coats on, and as a result, they get chilled in the freezing temperatures when they finally get outside. When they leave, they think, "I'm glad I finally made it out." And at the same time, Joe and Mary are thinking, "I thought they'd never leave!"

What has happened here is a problem common to many people. People do not know how to conclude gracefully. In this case, the conclusion is guests leaving a party or the hosts getting the last people out the door. Consequently, no one is happy with the situation. Of course, the lesson to be learned here is that when you say you are going to leave, do it. When someone else is having a hard time leaving, help them do it.

These same negative feelings can be created by speakers who say they are concluding and then do not keep their promise. In order to avoid negatives, make the conclusion brief. Be sure you have one, but **MAKE THE CONCLUSION BRIEF.** It is better to leave an audience wanting to hear more from you than to have them wish you would have finished sooner. Brevity is beneficial; long-windedness is detrimental.

There is a famous little saying that has been around for many years involving the steps followed by all good speakers: "Tell the audience what you're going to tell them, then tell them, and then tell them what you told them." The saying adequately illustrates the value of repetition by speakers who are well organized and carefully prepare an introduction and a conclusion for the body of their speeches.

At this stage in speech preparation, you have all the information you need to prepare the content of your speech. That content will slot into three large categories: introduction, body, and conclusion. The

"LIKE I SAID BEFORE, IN CONCLUSION..."

body will be the longest section and will make up about 75 to 80 percent of the speech. The introduction will take up about 15 to 20 percent, and the conclusion about 5 to 10 percent. These are approximations that vary slightly based on the speech content and individual speaker's personalities.

Now that you know all the parts in a speech, you will understand the importance of creating an outline to ensure good organization. Following is a sample outline for a speech, indicating the needed organization and desired repetition for a thesis containing three main ideas. The content of your speeches should follow this format, though (as you already know) the number of main ideas in the body may vary—based on time-limits and topic choice.

ORGANIZATIONAL OUTLINE FOR ALL SPEECHES

INTRODUCTION

    Grab attention

Establish relevance
Tell thesis   (Tell audience what you are going to tell them)

BODY   (Tell them)

   I. Restatement of first subdivision from thesis
     A. Supporting detail
     B. Supporting detail
     C. Supporting detail
  II. Restatement of second subdivision from thesis
     A. Supporting detail
     B. Supporting detail
     C. Supporting detail
 III. Restatement of third subdivision from thesis
     A. Supporting detail
     B. Supporting detail
     C. Supporting detail

CONCLUSION

End with finality
Name again subdivisions of thesis   (Tell them what you
                                            told them)
Denote power in last sentence

Now you know all the steps in preparing a speech, and we are now
ready to discuss that vital step that is so important after you have
written your speech—rehearsing your delivery.

10 *Rehearsing Your Delivery*

In the first chapter of this book, we discussed nervousness and ways to turn it to our advantage as a speaker. Though we now know that a certain level of nervous energy can be advantageous, we also know that too much nervousness can be a disadvantage. Quite simply, the easiest way to alleviate too much nervousness is to rehearse.

The single most common factor causing speakers to perform poorly is their failure to rehearse adequately. A speaker can fulfill the first several steps of creating a good speech, but all the hard work of those steps becomes nearly irrelevant to the actual speaking event *if the speaker has neglected to perform the last step—rehearsing.* All of the work of the previous steps is effectively undone by lack of adequately practicing the delivery.

When a speaker has rehearsed sufficiently before the actual performance, nervousness lessens as the speech progresses. The reverse is also true. When a speaker has not rehearsed enough before the actual performance, nervousness increases as the speech progresses.

Let's look at the steps you will follow in preparing your speech delivery.

Proofread Your Written Material Aloud and Revise

So far you have the content of your speech in writing, but the audience will not read an essay from you; rather they will only **hear** your words. Your job is to transform the written delivery into an oral one.

To accomplish this transformation, you must read your material aloud. You can do this in the privacy of your home. If you are bothered by others hearing you, read aloud from your bedroom, a study, the garage, the basement, an empty classroom, your car, or an office. The reason for reading aloud is that you can begin to discover where you will have problems pronouncing words. Change them to something easier to pronounce and simpler for the audience. You will also discover awkward and unclear areas that need to be simplified.

Nothing improves the written word more than speaking it aloud to discover flaws. Many writers use this technique for improving their writing; they know that reading the text aloud reveals poor word choice, awkward sentence structure, and weaknesses in logic. If this is true for writers, it is a hundred times more true for the speaker.

Remember that a speaker's audience has a chance to hear the spoken word only once. Once that sentence is spoken, they never again hear it. If they have a difficult time understanding the spoken words, they cannot go back and look at them again to decipher the meaning, as they could do with the written word. So it is crucial that you revise the wording for the sake of both you and your audience.

You will need to read it aloud three or four times, revising it each time.

Time the Speech

The next step in getting ready to rehearse your delivery is to read it aloud with the improvements you have made and, in addition, timing it. You need to use the stopwatch feature on your watch (if it has one), a microwave oven timer, a stove timer, or an alarm clock. Set the timer to go off in the time requirements of your speech.

If your beginning speeches are to be four to six minutes long, set the timer for five minutes. The reason you want to aim for the middle time slot is that most speakers tend to get nervous and speed up in the actual delivery in front of an audience. Aiming for the middle slot allows for that deviation. Likewise, there are a few speakers who slow down during the actual delivery. If you do not know what your tendencies are, this timing method allows for either occurrence without harming your time requirements.

Usually, you will discover your material is not yet within the correct time limitations. The best position to be in is to have too much material and have to knock some out. The reason having too much is more desirable than having too little is because with too much, all you have to do is cut what is in front of you. If you have too little material, you have to go back to the library to do additional researching and reading. Having to find more material is much more time consuming than eliminating already existent information.

A further advantage of having too much material is that you can now choose the very best from what is available. Some of your examples and illustrations will not be as interesting as others. These are the ones you want to eliminate. You want to select your material based on how well it explains and supports your main ideas and, at the same time, provides interest and relevance. Having extra material allows you to fulfill these obligations to your listeners.

Being within the specified time limitations is extremely important and is the area most often breached by speakers. Let's look at what happens when someone speaks for too long.

Remember the discussion about speech conclusions that do not fulfill the speaker's promises to end the speech? The audience "sits on pins and needles," shifting around, bored and resentful that the speaker is still droning on and on. The same idea is true for the whole speech. Whenever people attend a program to hear speakers, they usually have a program that indicates each speaker's time slot. Otherwise, the program, the convention, the seminar, or the panel forum will not finish as scheduled.

Let me show you the repercussions of a speaker not fulfilling his or her time obligations to an audience. In a large city in the Midwest, a neurological convention was scheduled for a whole day at a hotel. The speakers were all medical doctors who had researched in various areas of neurology, and the morning session consisted of several doctors, each of whom was to deliver a presentation for 30 minutes. Several registered nurses paid to attend this convention, and several of them told me they especially wanted to hear the last speaker on the list of the morning session. However, the next-to-the-last speaker, after his 30 minutes were past, was still going strong. After he had gone beyond his time-frame by 10 minutes, the moderator (who introduced each speaker), walked to the podium and mentioned that he was well over his time limit and must sit down. He responded apologetically and said he would finish with a few final words. Ten minutes later, he finished. The last doctor was visibly angry and had only ten minutes to give her presentation. Hence she had to cut her speech by two thirds of its contents because of someone who did not abide by the obligations of timing, which comes through rehearsing.

The view the nurses had of the long-winded speaker was that he was selfish, and they are correct. He did not care that he had been given a time slot to adhere to, he did not care that another medical colleague was forced to delete most of her speech, and he did not care that those who needed the last doctor's information did not get it. He had wasted other people's time, an infringement that poor speakers are notorious for.

When an audience expects a speaker to fall within a given time period, that speaker better fulfill his or her obligation, or risk being labeled selfish and inconsiderate of others. A bad impression is hard for a speaker to overcome, because people do not forget someone who does not care about them.

Good speakers leave the audience when all is going well so that the listeners want to hear them again. This positive impression cannot be made unless the speaker is within the time limits.

You will need to continue reading your speech aloud and revising it until it falls within the time limits.

Rehearse From Note Cards or an Outline

After you have revised the written form of your speech and know that the reading of it falls within the required timing, it is time for you either to place key words of that speech onto note cards or to create an outline on paper. Do not write your entire speech on the note cards or outline, though. Otherwise, you will be doing a manuscript reading from the full text, and you are to be giving an extemporaneous delivery (Chapter 3).

This type of delivery means you will have key words and phrases on note cards and will deliver the ideas around those words. The wording you use will be your own, not memorized (as in memorized delivery), not impromptu (without notes or previous preparation), and not manuscript reading (reading the whole text verbatim). The advantages of extemporaneous delivery is that it sounds conversational, yet is organized so the audience can easily follow the main ideas.

At first as you try to deliver your speech from the notes, you will falter and stammer and stumble. That's typical of any speaker. What you must do is revamp your notes until you know that you have the most important words on them. It is likely you will revise them three or four times, if not more. Put all key ideas on these cards, as well as any phrases or areas you keep forgetting. The cards are for you, not your audience. So keep revising them with your delivery in mind. Capitalize some words, highlight some with magic marker, place slashes where you want to pause. Personalize them until you can deliver the speech smoothly from them within the specified time limits.

An error that beginning speakers sometimes make is that they wait until the last minute to transfer their full text to the outline form. Then when they get in front of the audience, they verbally stumble around because the notes are so different from the written manuscript that they cannot deliver a smooth speech. **As soon as possible,** transfer your ideas to cards or to an outline so that your rehearsals will reflect exactly the formal delivery.

A second error is that a few rare individuals like to chat in front of groups. So this type of person figures he or she is not going to be nervous and then gets in front of the group and talks on and on and on, going way outside the time limits and cutting other speakers out of that day's schedule. Lots of enemies are made that way, and a very negative speaking reputation is established in one fell swoop!

One thing you might want to do if you use note cards is to label one note card "Introduction," the subdivisions of the thesis "Body," and the last one, "Conclusion." Also, you will number your cards so you can easily put them in order. If you use a full-page outline, you will want to use indenting and double spacing between lines so you can easily glance at the page and find your place. In addition, I personally use capitalization of key words, different colors of highlighters for different emphasis, and a slash mark (/) wherever I want a pause for effect. My advice is always to write out the full first sentence of the introduction. You may have a dandy attention grabber in that first sentence and think you will never forget it, but as soon as you get in front of a group of staring eyes, you can forget some surprising things, including your own name! By having the first sentence written, you can pause initially to make sure you remember it correctly and then look straight at the listeners' eyes and deliver it. This "safety technique" gives you the self-confidence and the courage to know that all will go as planned. The beginning is very, very important for both you and your audience. Do everything you can to make it strong. The other full sentence you should have as a "security blanket" in your notes is the thesis statement. Similarly, be sure to have that powerful last sentence written out just for safekeeping.

If you forget that last line, you will have a very clumsy ending and harm the speech. Be sure to look straight at the audience when you deliver the last line; eye contact heightens the power of the delivery.

The rest of the material in the notes will have phrases and words that help you remember what comes next in the speech. Any quotations from other sources should be very short and written out. Most of the time you will put someone else's ideas in your own words and then tell the source of the information. The minimum information is the name of the source and why the person is an expert; where you got the information; and the year the article or book was written, the program was aired, or the expert was interviewed. Look back at Chapter 7 to see how the supporting details on stress give credit to the sources.

Below is the self-introduction speech from Chapter 8. Following the full text are sample note cards for the speech and then a sample full-sentence outline for the same speech.

Full Text of Self-Introduction Speech

You and I have a lot in common. We are after the same basic goal, a degree in our chosen major. You think your major will ultimately make you happy. I hope you are right, but I am more fortunate than some of you because I do not just *THINK* my major will make me happy; I *KNOW* because it already has brought me much happiness. The reason I know that I will be happy with my major is because of my experiences that I am about to share with you. You will be able to remember me because of my name, my employer, and my interests and how they are all interconnected.

First, my name is one that is easy to remember because the first and last are alike. My name came about because my parents (like some of yours) named me after another relative—in this case, my grandfather. But they also wanted one that was simple. I think that resulted from the fact that my father's first and middle name is Maurice Maynard. Not only isn't that an easy name but also people hear the first name and write it incorrectly. They write it "Morris" as in the famous television cat, Morris. So Dad simplifies matters and goes by the nickname Mac. Similar to my father's difficult name, my mother's first and middle name is Hattie Marie; she so much hates her name that almost no one knows her real name because she has always gone by the name Pat. And, no, I have no idea how she got the name Pat out of Hattie Marie. Well, so far, you know my name is not going to be Maurice or Maynard, and it certainly isn't Hattie or Marie. My name (first and last) is Sammy Sams. Simple, isn't it? Actually, the correct name is Samuel Sams (after my mother's father), but even as a child, I was christened with the shortened form Sammy Sams. Some people tell me it sounds like a stage name. Even so, acting is not what Sammy Sams is interested in doing with his life.

What I am interested in doing with my life, I am already doing where I am employed part time. My employer not only makes me happy but also serves as a way for you to remember my name. Oddly enough I am employed at Good Samaritan Hospital. Yes, Sammy Sams works at Good Sam. As humorous as this may sound to you (and I admit it is unusual), I am very serious about my employment as an assistant in the physical therapy department. This work I do to help others rehabilitate their muscles and gain full use of their limbs makes me happy. I gain fulfillment when I watch someone who has been injured set aside crutches and take the first small steps to recuperation. I feel happy inside when I watch a victim of an accident overcome inability to use an arm or hand. I have seen smiles appear on faces that moments before revealed pain; I have seen tears of happiness replace tears of sadness; I have witnessed success by someone using a limb after she had been told she would never be able to use it again! Yes, my job at Good Sam brings me great joy, and I am here at this college to gain more training in physical therapy because I know it will help me gain ground on my road to happiness.

Now you know that Sammy Sams works at Good Sam, but you do not know my interests outside of my job. Though I have many, I am going to share with you just one—one that is interconnected to my job. One of my outside interests is giving my time as a volunteer to an organization called Riding For The Handicapped. This organization offers physically or mentally handicapped children and adults the chance to increase their abilities by experiencing horseback riding. The theory behind Riding For The Handicapped is that sometimes when traditional rehabilitation therapy (such as that in a hospital) fails, a nontraditional one may not. Frequently, participation in sports is assumed to be impossible for someone with extreme physical or mental limitations; however, teachers in this program believe that the excitement of petting a horse and of feeling a horse's muscles working beneath a handicapped rider whose muscles do not work so well will do two things: one, it will excite the rider when the realization "hits" that he or she will be riding a horse regularly, and two, actually riding the horse allows the rider to feel the horse's muscles at work. As with my job in physical therapy, I have experienced wonderful success stories. Once I watched as a rider could not sit on the horse without being held on by the two spotters; that is, one person on the left of the saddle and one on the right are always available to catch or support a rider. This particular rider, Joe, had been riding for eight weeks and had to be held up by the two spotters; I was one of those spotters. During the ninth week, Joe seemed to be riding rather well, and the teachers motioned me and the other spotter to let go of him. We cautiously did, and there was Joe sitting in the saddle and riding a horse without any help. I'll never forget Joe's laugh when he realized what had happened, and I'll never forget the tears in his mother's eyes as she watched a miracle occur. My combining traditional physical therapy at a hospital with nontraditional therapy as a volunteer for Riding For The Handicapped allows me options about how to best help people overcome their limitations.

Sammy Sams may sound like a stage name, but my job at Good Sam and my volunteering for Riding For The Handicapped are more exciting to me than acting. Rather than performing a make-believe scene with make-believe heroes, I am helping ordinary people in real-life scenes, and I am watching them turn real-life handicaps and tragedies into heroic accomplishments and real-life miracles.

SAMPLE NOTE CARDS

INTRODUCTION   1

    You and I have a lot in common.
       Same basic goal—degree
       Think—be happy
       Hope you're right.
    I'm fortunate—I DON'T THINK; I KNOW
    The reason . . . I will share

**THESIS: YOU WILL BE ABLE TO REMEMBER ME
BECAUSE OF MY NAME, MY EMPLOYER, AND MY
INTERESTS—AND HOW THEY ARE ALL INTER-
CONNECTED.**

BODY—I. EASY NAME   2

    Name = easy . . . First and Last
      —Named after grandfather
      —ALSO name to be simple
         Father's name . . .
            People hear first and write wrong
            TV cat
            Nickname—MAC

SAMPLE NOTE CARDS (Continued)

BODY—I. EASY NAME (Continued)   3

    Like Dad's name, Mom's name
      She Hates it
      No one knows her real one
      Nickname—Pat
   No, I don't know how she got Pat out of . . .
   SO FAR YOU KNOW MY NAME ISN'T . . . AND
CERTAINLY NOT . . . !
   My name is . . . Some say it's STAGE NAME . . .
   EVEN SO, ACTING IS NOT WHAT . . .

BODY—II. EMPLOYMENT   4

   What I am interested in . . . I am already doing
   MY EMPLOYER NOT ONLY MAKES ME HAPPY BUT
ALSO SERVES AS A WAY FOR YOU TO REMEMBER MY
NAME.
   Good Samaritan . . . . Yes, S S at Good Sam.
   —Sounds humorous—is unusual, but . . . Serious abt job.
   —Work to rehabilitate . . . makes me happy.
   —Gain fulfillment when . . . injured set aside crutches
   —Happy inside when . . . accident victim uses arm/hand

SAMPLE NOTE CARDS (Continued)

BODY—II. EMPLOYMENT (Continued)   5

   —Have seen smiles on . . . faces . . . before = pain
   —have seen tears of happiness replace . . . sadness
   —have witnessed success . . . use limb when told never . . .

YES, MY JOB AT GOOD SAM = JOY, AND I'M HERE AT . . .
TO GAIN MORE TRAINING IN PT BECAUSE I KNOW
IT WILL HELP ME GAIN GROUND ON ROAD TO
HAPPINESS.

BODY—III. INTERESTS OUTSIDE OF JOB   6

   Now you know that Sammy Sams works at . . . but don't
know interests outside of job.

   Have many . . . but share one-one interconnected to job.
   —Outside interest . . . give time to org. R for H
   —This org. . . . offers . . . children & adults . . .
   —Theory behind R for H (traditional vs Non-)
     —sports participation = impossible
   however/

SAMPLE NOTE CARDS (Continued)

BODY—III. INTERESTS OUTSIDE OF JOB (Continued)   7

—Teachers believe petting horse/feeling muscle
    2 advantages:
        1. excite & motivate
        2. transfer muscle movement concept
—As with employment, success stories here . . .
    Once, rider needed 2 spotters (explain)
    Joe, in 9th wk, spotters told to let go
        —Joe's laugh; mother's tears

Combining traditional & non- = options for me on helping . . .

CONCLUSION   8

    SS . . . stage name, but job . . . and volunteer work =
more exciting than acting.

RATHER THAN PERFORMING A MAKE-BELIEVE
SCENE WITH MAKE-BELIEVE HEROES, I AM HELPING
ORDINARY PEOPLE IN REAL-LIFE SCENES, AND I AM
WATCHING THEM TURN REAL-LIFE HANDICAPS &
TRAGEDIES INTO HEROIC ACCOMPLISHMENTS &
REAL-LIFE MIRACLES.

SAMPLE FULL-SENTENCE OUTLINE FOR SELF-INTRODUCTION
(Follows outline format from the end of Chapter 9)

Introduction:

Attention: (Pause) You and I have a lot in common.
Relevance: We are after the same goal, a degree. You think
                your major will make you happy. I not only think,
                but rather I know mine will.
Thesis: You will be able to remember me because of my
                name, my employer, and my interests and how
                they are all interconnected.

BODY

    I. First, my name is one that is easy to remember because the
       first and last are alike.
       A. Name came about from grandfather.
       B. Name needed to be simple.
       C. Give my father's name.
          1. Tell about spelling.
          2. Tell about nickname.
       D. Give my mother's name.
          1. She hates it.
          2. No one knows real name.
          3. She gave herself nickname; I have no idea how she
             arrived at it.
       E. So far you know my name isn't Dad's or Mom's.
       F. My name is Sammy Sams—(simple).
(Concluding Sent.) Even though some say it's a stage name, acting
isn't what Sammy Sams wants.
    II. What I am interested in doing with my life, I am already doing
       where I am employed part-time.
       A. My job not only makes me happy but also helps you
          remember my name.
       B. Oddly enough, I am employed at Good Samaritan.
       C. As humorous and unusual as it sounds, I am serious
          about my job in PT.

    D. Helping others rehabilitate muscles and limbs makes
       me happy.
      1. I gain fulfillment when I watch the injured set aside
         crutches and take small steps.
      2. I feel happy inside when I watch a victim of an accident
         overcome inability.
      3. I have seen smiles appear where pain was.
      4. I have seen tears of happiness replace tears of sadness.
      5. I have witnessed success by someone using a limb after
         being told they wouldn't.

(Concluding Sent.) Yes, my job at Good Sam brings joy, and I am
here to gain more training in PT because I know it will help me
gain ground on my road to happiness.

   III. Now you know Sammy Sams works at Good Sam, but you do
      not know my outside interests. Though I have many, I am
      going to share just one—interconnected to my job—and that
      is volunteering for the organization Riding For The Handi-
      capped.
    A. Riding For The Hanidcapped offers handicapped the
       chance to increase abilities by horseback riding.
    B. The theory behind it is when traditional therapy doesn't
       work, nontraditional may.
      1. Traditionalists believe sports are impossible for severely
         handicapped.
      2. Teachers in Riding For The Handicapped believe excite-
         ment of petting horses and feeling muscles while riding
         helps with use of rider's muscle use.
      3. I experienced success of rider needing two "spotters";
         I was one.
        a. Joe rode for eight weeks.
        b. In ninth week, teachers motioned us to let go.
        c. I'll never forget Joe's laugh and his mother's tears a
          the miracle.

(Concluding Sent.) My combining traditional physical therapy at a
hospital with nontraditional therapy as a volunteer for Riding For
The Handicapped allows me options about how to best help people
overcome their limitations.

CONCLUSION

Finality:	Sammy Sams may sound like a stage name, but
Thesis:	my job at Good Sam and volunteering at Riding For The Handicapped gives me options for helping people.
Last Sentence:	Rather than performing a make-believe scene with make-believe heroes, I am helping ordinary people in real-life scenes, and I am watching them turn real-life handicaps and tragedies into heroic accomplishments and real-life miracles.

These sample notes help you see how to prepare your notes from the full text of a speech. Keep in mind that each individual will vary as to what words will go on the cards or the outline. And the notes will be revised after the first few rehearsals, until the speaker can speak smoothly from the notes. If you keep having trouble remembering a line or section you really want to deliver, then you will put that on your note cards or outline as extra help. Note cards and outlines should contain main ideas and key words of examples, but they are always individualized according to each speaker's needs. The full-sentence outline above is a detailed outline; some outlines are less detailed; keep in mind, however, less on paper means more must be remembered by the speaker. On the other hand, such a detailed outline as the one above has the detriment of providing too much of a "crutch" for the speaker and can cause a lack of eye contact with the audience. My personal favorite is the use of cards, but there are those who dislike cards and prefer full outline form. Ultimately, **with enough practice,** either one will work. The key is to practice enough not to have to rely on any notes too heavily.

Practice Good Delivery Techniques

Though there are various elements of a good delivery, there are five key areas to consciously practice.

1. Voice

Surely you have heard speakers who talk in monotone, barely changing their pitch or word emphasis during a whole speech. Speaking in a monotone puts an audience to sleep and shows that the speaker is not excited about the content of the speech. If the speaker isn't interested, how could an audience be interested?

I have often walked by people standing in groups of peers, talking about their past weekend's activities or their plans for a party or some interesting incident. They are full of energy and vocal variety. Their listeners are enjoying the storyteller and laugh and gasp in appropriate places. All are enjoying the communication event. Later I have seen these same individuals get in front of a group to deliver a formal speech, and all of a sudden there is no vocal variety, no excitement, no energy—just monotone lines. These lines are received with the same enthusiasm as they are given. If a speaker is not interested in the speech, neither will the audience be interested. If a speaker is enjoying the content of the speech, the energy will come through the vocal cords, and the audience will "catch" the enthusiasm of the speaker.

To verify the effectiveness of vocal variety, all we need to do is listen to a mother or father telling a fairy tale to a two-year-old child. The parent's voice becomes gruffer or kinder, louder or softer, scarier or calmer—according to the plot of the story. And the child's facial expression follows every animated word and gesture, an attentive audience reacting vividly to the speaker. What a shame that we believe as adults that we are supposed to lose all that wonderful, natural vocal animation. The natural listener's reaction is that of the child, and true to human nature, our audiences react according to our willingness to get involved. Our involvement (or lack of it) shows through our voice.

One of the best techniques for checking your voice is to tape yourself on a cassette recorder. Play it back and listen objectively. Pretend it is someone else. Did this person sound interested in the speech? Was there adequate vocal variety and word emphasis? Or was the speech in a narrow vocal range, bordering on monotone. Work on improving vocal delivery. A note of caution: Though rare, it is possible to overdo vocal variety by greatly exaggerating and going outside normal boundaries. It is perfectly permissible to go to extremes while reading to a small child, but that same exuberance would obviously be negatively viewed by an adult audience.

2. Grammar/Pronunciation/Enunciation

One of the differences in delivering a public speech and talking to a small group of friends is that one is organized in advance and rehearsed, and the other is organized on the spot and spontaneous. When a speech is rehearsed as a public speaking occasion, the words are carefully chosen with the audience in mind, avoiding slang and terminology. Also, correct grammar should be used, and words should be fully pronounced. This includes the *-ed* and *-ing* endings on words. In everyday informal speech, we tend to drop endings and sometimes not fully pronounce words, which is fine for the occasion. The occasion, however, changes when we speak publicly, and our handling of the language should change to match the more formal occasion.

3. Pauses/Rate

Another reason to tape your speech as you practice it is to discover your speaking speed. Listeners tend to listen better if the rate of speech is at a fairly fast clip. So, when you rehearse, you should not intentionally pause between words and talk more slowly than normal speech. This behavior causes listeners to believe they are being treated as if they are not intelligent, and they become irritated. If you practice at any different pace than your normal speaking rate, you should speed up a little, which maintains audience interest.

One caution when you practice at a fast rate is not to sound like you are racing. You are not in a contest to see how fast you can talk; you are merely increasing the overall rate a little. Likewise, you do not want to hold the exact same pace for every sentence. In our everyday speech, we say some sentences at a fast pace and some at a slower pace. You will want to have some variation within the speech to reflect a normal pattern.

One bad habit that can develop (as a speaker tries to word the next sentence) is repeating pet phrases, such as "uh," "um," "you know," and "see what I mean." The best way to avoid incorporating such habits is to tape-record yourself and listen for any repetitions. Then you can immediately begin working on eliminating them.

One thing you will want to plan intentionally that is not part of a normal pattern is pausing. Silence can sometimes be deafening. It is an effective tool to call attention to some very important idea or to let a poignant story sink into the listeners' minds. So plan pauses where you want some key ideas to be remembered. Do not plan too many, though, or they will lose their power.

4. Eye Contact

If there is one single factor that I consider to be the most vital in a speaking situation, it is eye contact. Some of my students of speech tell me they heard that one way to get out of making eye contact was to stare above the heads of the audience. Whenever I am told this in a classroom situation, I proceed to talk for the next two or three minutes staring above everyone's head. The reaction is always the same. Since I usually have strong eye contact, the sudden reduction of it to zero is the strongest message I can send. The listeners laugh and immediately get the point: Communication is reduced to almost nothing, and the audience knows they are not important enough to look at.

Having little or no eye contact is uncomfortable for the audience and harms any attempts at communicating effectively. Would you expect a basketball player to shoot without looking at the basket? Would you expect a golfer to hit the ball without watching it? Would you expect a pianist never to look at the keys? A speaker's purpose is to communicate with the audience, and therefore to avoid eye contact is to avoid communication.

In some public speaking situations, it is not possible to look at the eyes of every audience member. The best policy is to look at a person's eyes for three or four seconds and then to look at someone else. Do not merely glance from one person to another. Realize that you are looking at individual people, and talk to that person momentarily before moving to someone else. In addition, be sure that you look at someone on the far left of the room, in the middle, and on the far right. Look at someone near the front, halfway back, and then in the rear. That way you include everyone, even though you cannot look at each one individually. I recommend that you practice in front of a room and pretend there are many listeners in front of you. Rehearse by looking at various areas at about the height of a person's eyes. In that way, you will have some idea of what your physical actions will be at the actual performance. There is one problem you need to be aware of: Sometimes when a beginning speaker notices one person in the audience who is listening very attentively, the speaker begins looking at only that one individual. It feels so good to know that someone is really listening that the rest of the listeners are ignored. Be careful of this temptation, for it harms communication with all but the one individual. Look at several in the audience, not just one or two.

Lastly, you will hear conflicting views as to the value of practicing by looking into a mirror. Each person must decide for him- or herself. However, I see the advantages, at some point in your practice, of rehearsing in front of a room as if you have listeners present. The reason is simply that you are not going to be looking into a mirror when you deliver the speech to the audience. You are going to be looking into the eyes of people throughout the audience. If you rehearse it in a setting as close as possible to the one you will actually have when you perform, you are less likely to feel uncomfortable. Along with this reasoning, I would like to propose that when you look into a mirror, you are concentrating on yourself, a very egocentric emphasis and one that opposes the function of communication—to share ideas with others. If you concentrate on your message, emphasize your audience, and de-emphasize yourself, you will be less likely to make embarrassing errors (since you are not concentrating on the negative possibilities) and more likely to succeed in interesting your audience (since you are concentrating on them and how they receive your message).

I know that you are aware of the value of eye contact. When you see someone who is attractive to you, what is the first thing you do but try to establish eye contact. When you want to know whether someone is pleased with you or angry at you, what is the first thing you check but eyes and facial expression. Nonverbal facial signals tell us what a person is feeling. In fact, when words and actions do not match up in meaning, it is the person's nonverbal signals that most often indicate truthful feelings; this contradiction between words and actions gave birth to the saying, "Actions speak louder than words." The eyes and face are the first source of communication with another.

5. Gestures/Movement

If you do not feel natural making gestures and moving nearer the audience, then do not do either until you can do so naturally. Otherwise, your gestures will look artificial and planned, which takes away from your believability. An audience is less likely to notice no gestures than they are to notice awkward, ill-timed movements. After speaking a few times, you will begin to relax enough to concentrate on the message and the audience, and then you will begin using your natural gestures.

The major problem confronting speakers usually does not involve too little movement but rather too much movement. Nervous energy can sometimes result in the following nervous actions that can become habits unless they are caught and curbed:

A. Pacing back and forth
B. Wagging one foot or leg
C. Tapping a foot or heel
D. Drumming fingers on the rostrum
E. Playing with a ring, or watch, or hair
F. Removing and replacing glasses
G. Jangling change in pockets
H. Shuffling your notes (Many beginning speakers lose their places this way!)

The basic rule about movement and gestures is that any movement that calls attention to itself and does not help the content of what is being said should be avoided; any movement that helps the audience remember the speaker's content is good, purposeful movement.

An extreme incident of nervousness was told to me by another speech teacher. He said that during a speech performance, a beginning speaker had unbuttoned his whole shirt and then rebuttoned it before the finish. When the speaker was informed about his nervous activity, he thought the teacher and the audience were joking and didn't believe he had done it. Fortunately, the speaker was not a female, and also fortunately, this is a rare and extreme example of extraneous movement that can result from the energy produced by the fear of speaking. Practice helps prevent needless movements.

Furthermore, I would encourage you to practice the walk to the front of the audience and the walk back to your seat. I don't recall seeing such a suggestion before, but nervousness is at its height during that "fifty-mile" walk to the front. If you rehearse getting out of a chair, carrying your note cards and visuals, placing them where you want them, and pausing before beginning, you will feel more natural when the actual performance occurs.

In addition, before entering the room on the day of your speech, go to the rest room and look yourself over. Check your apparel, your face, your hair, your teeth, and spit out your gum. Never attempt a speech with gum in your mouth. Checking yourself beforehand is your insurance against the fear of embarrassment that so many speakers have. A last-minute overview adds to your feeling of self-confidence; you know beyond a doubt that your appearance is as you want it to be.

When you practice standing in front of the audience, consciously position yourself in ways that will "keep you out of trouble." That is, planting both your feet on the floor and equally distributing body weight over each leg will stop you from having one leg loose to wiggle, and it will stop the possibility of a foot beginning a toe-tapping routine. Putting each hand on the side of the rostrum or podium will stop you from tapping your fingers, playing with jewelry, or shuffling your note cards.

Likewise, you should practice gathering the materials after the speech is finished and then walking back to your chair. The important point to remember is that the audience is gaining an impression from you all this time, so it is important that you remain poised and in control.

One common error repeated by speakers is that near the end of their speech, they begin gathering their materials and walking to their seat before they are done talking. That last sentence is to be powerful and leave the audience thinking about the topic. Power is lost when the speaker looks too eager to sit down. The premature movement to leave the audience emphasizes that you are more interested in getting away from the audience than communicating with them.

As you can see, the delivery is a very complex part of the speech and requires a great deal of time. If you spent eight hours preparing a speech but fail to rehearse it, you negate all those hours of work. On the other hand, if you spend several different sessions rehearsing your speech, you are likely to become an effective speaker.

One of the ways you can increase the power of your presentation is by using visual aids. Your use of these aids, however, can be either detrimental or beneficial. Both the negatives and the positives of visual aids are discussed in the next chapter.

11 Providing Visual Aids

Visual aids include **anything visual.** If a speaker wears clothing relating to the speech topic and refers to it during the speech, the clothing becomes a visual aid. If the speaker writes on the chalkboard, the audience sees a visual aid. If the speaker uses his or her hands to show the approximate size of something, then the use of a visual aid has occurred. Beyond what has been named, visual aids include posters, enlarged pictures, magazines, objects, slides, overhead transparencies, and videos.

Visual aids should be used whenever possible because they affect both our sense of sight and our sense of hearing. If, in addition, the speaker involves the audience by having them physically do something, the sense of touch is affected. The more senses that the speaker can affect, the more involved the audience becomes. The more involved the audience becomes, the more effective the communication.

It is important, however, to analyze your audience carefully before deciding to involve them. For example, it becomes an unwieldy task to get a whole audience involved in aerobic exercise, and the speaker can often lose control because some audience members may begin laughing and talking. Furthermore, some will not appreciate being forced into such types of activity. Another activity that frequently does not work well is trying to get all listeners to close their eyes. The

134

problems here are (1) inevitably some will not cooperate and (2) the speaker loses the advantages of eye contact.

Though you might assume visual aids are always positive, a balance must be achieved so that negatives do not occur. If you make the assumption that the more visual aids you use, the better the speech will be, you will show you do not know the purpose of a visual aid.

Use Visual Aids to Provide Emphasis

A visual aid is used for emphasis. The desired result may be to create impact, facilitate understanding, increase comprehension, or simplify data. Whatever the reason for the use of visual aids, their goal is to emphasize some aspect of the speech. The definition of *emphasize* is to "accentuate, intensify, or provide prominence." If a speaker uses numerous visual aids throughout the whole speech, nothing is given prominence. If everything is emphasized, then no two or three are accentuated, but rather all is the same weight; hence, nothing is emphasized. To be accentuated, an item must stand out from the others. The point is that a speaker can use too many visual aids and defeat their purpose; there is a point of diminishing returns. Decide what you want to emphasize or dramatize, and then use the visual aids accordingly and sparingly.

Learn to Create and Display Visual Aids Appropriately

Anytime a craftsperson gets new tools of the trade, he or she must learn how to use them and then practice using them to their fullest advantage. Consider visual aids the tools of a speaker's craft. Their proper use falls under four large categories: appearance, instruction, distribution, and showing.

1. Appearance

Whatever visual you decide to use must be easy for your audience to see.

If you decide to create a poster, you need to consider the size of the poster and the size of the print from each listener's point of view. It must have large enough print to be easily read by every single person in the audience. A group of thirty or forty can see a large poster, but an audience consisting of more than forty probably will not easily see it. Below is a personal experience of what can happen if you do not create visual aids of proper size.

On one speaking occasion, one of my beginning speakers turned around his visual aid to show the audience. The aid was about the size of an 8 X 11 sheet of paper and contained fifteen numbered items, each a full, long, hand-printed sentence. The poster was filled from top to bottom and from side to side. When the speaker set the poster in front of the rostrum and pointed to the first item, someone in the audience chuckled. The size of the print couldn't even be seen by those right in front of it. The absurdity of the situation was accentuated by one infectious chuckle, which spread like an epidemic. Soon the audience was in mass hysteria, and I (who pride myself in being calm and collected in the unusual situations that public speaking often presents)—yes, I also lost control and joined in laughter. I had to stop the speaker, dismiss the class, and sit and talk with the wounded spirit of a beginning speaker. The speech would have been an undeniable success had it only been about how **not** to use visual aids. Unfortunately, that was not the topic. When the speaker was given a second chance, he vastly improved his use of visual aids.

Let's suppose I want to speak on the "don'ts" of a speech introduction, as listed in Chapter 9. If I take the listing and modify it on a poster as follows and make the print large enough for all to see, I have still committed a major error: I have listed too much material on my visual.

VISUAL CONTAINING TOO MUCH INFORMATION

"DON'TS OF A SPEECH INTRODUCTION"

1. Don't endanger an audience
2. Don't make a speech introduction so intense that it overpowers the rest of what you say. (The goal is to get the audience to listen **to what follows** the introduction.)

(Continued)

VISUAL CONTAINING TOO MUCH INFORMATION (Continued)

3. Don't use introductory content that is not related to your speech topic.
4. Don't use any material that might offend any member of the audience. If you think a joke might insult anyone, don't use it. If you have a short anecdote that might be taken in a negative way, avoid telling it. Remember the following simple rule:
   ## WHEN IN DOUBT, DON'T.
5. Don't let the first words out of your mouth be "Today, I'm going to tell you ..." or some such similar statement. We've already established your first words should be something that grabs audience attention and is unique to your topic. The words above are so general that every speaker in the world could use them for any topic; such a beginning has no uniqueness or interest factor.
6. Don't assume your audience will laugh at what you think is funny. If you have a sense of humor and feel at ease using it in a speech, keep in mind that not everyone thinks the same thing is funny. So if you use humor, plan it as if you do not expect the audience to laugh.

Now we can make an improvement by reducing all the excess wording except for the main ideas.

IMPROVEMENT OF VISUAL AID ABOVE

"DON'TS OF A SPEECH INTRODUCTION"

1. Don't endanger an audience.
2. Don't make a speech introduction so intense that it overpowers the rest of what you say.
3. Don't use introductory content that is not related to your speech topic.
4. Don't use any material that might offend any member of the audience.
5. Don't let the first words out of your mouth be "Today, I'm going to tell you ..." or some such similar statement.
6. Don't assume your audience will laugh at what you think is funny.

Though the above is an improvement, six full sentences should not be on a visual aid. Remember, a visual aid is for emphasis; the speaker

---

MORE IMPROVEMENT FOR VISUAL AID

"DON'TS OF A SPEECH INTRODUCTION"

1. ENDANGER AUDIENCE
2. CREATE ATTENTION-GETTER OVERPOWERING THE BODY
3. USE ATTENTION-GETTER UNRELATED TO TOPIC
4. PRESENT OFFENSIVE MATERIAL
5. ELIMINATE ATTENTION-GETTER
6. ASSUME PARALLEL SENSE OF HUMOR WITH AUDIENCE

---

will not stop talking when showing the visual aid, but uses the aid to emphasize a major point and to help the audience understand and remember the key information. Hence, the next visual is still another improvement because it does not use full sentences.

With the above improved visual aid, the speaker could point at each number and discuss the meaning with the audience. There are some, however, who would claim that having six items listed on the same poster, no matter how short, are too many. One problem is that while the speaker is pointing to one, some audience members are looking at the others. To remedy this potential problem, the speaker can buy small poster boards that are about eighteen inches square and have a single item on each. As each is discussed, that poster is put up for the audience to view. When the next poster is put up, it is placed on top of the previous one; then each point remains isolated.

Another possibility is that a picture might be created from some of the individual listings; the impact of a relevant picture is enormous. Remember the old line "A picture paints a thousand words." Look at the pictures on pages 139 and 140 representing Point 1 and Point 6 from the list above.

Of all the visuals that have been presented, which is the most likely to be remembered? The simpler the visual aid in terms of audience comprehension, the more powerful and memorable the impact.

2. Instruction

A speaker must give instruction to the audience about the visual aid. Put another way, a speaker must never assume the audience un-

"TO DEMONSTRATE THE SMALL AMOUNT OF TIME BEFORE EXPLOSION AFTER PULLING THE PIN FROM THE HAND GRENADE..."

Point 1 as a Picture

derstands the visual aid or will read it on their own. It is the speaker's job to point to each part of the aid as it is discussed and to explain it fully in relation to the topic.

Never give a silent demonstration or a silent showing of a visual aid. If you give a demonstration, you must keep talking as you show how to do each of the steps for whatever process you are demonstrating. You are obligated to keep informing the audience, adding additional interesting information about your topic. If whatever you want to demonstrate takes too long for the time limitations, then do some of those time-consuming steps outside the speaking situation so you can show larger finished steps to the audience, explaining how long the process would normally take. That way the audience sees the demonstration and also sees several completed steps without having to wait.

Similarly, the amount of information on a visual aid can limit understanding rather than foster it. Too much information is confusing to an audience and takes too long for the speaker to explain. A long

Point 6 as a Picture

series of numbers is too complicated either with a visual aid or without one. Explanation of a formula in simple terms with an enlarged example is appropriate.

I have had beginning speakers use an overhead transparency filled with sentences or numbers from top to bottom. In fact, David Peoples, international speaker and sales trainer for major corporations, states, "The world's worst visual aid is a black-and-white transparency of a typewritten page."[1] There isn't time in a full hour to cover that much information even if the audience could read it, which they can't. The speaker would be more effective to show the whole sheet briefly, take it away, and then say, "I'm going to show you only one line of this sheet, enlarged so it is easy to see, and demonstrate how to apply the formula to it. The rest of the lines follow this identical process." The purpose of a visual is to enhance understanding. That occurs with simplification and narrowing to one instance, not with reams of numbers or sentences.

Remember that the visual aid is just that: an aid and a help to the speaker's **words.**

3. Distribution

A beginning speaker should not distribute anything to the audience. At some point in time, a speaker will want to hand out copies of a page or else pass an object around the class. It might be good advice to consider the "D," which begins the word "distribution" is also the beginning for the word "Disadvantages."

The disadvantages of passing something around the audience are so great that rarely are they overcome by anything advantageous. Let's look at the situation more closely.

When a speaker shows a small object, which indeed cannot be seen by the whole audience, the temptation is to pass it around, so the speaker walks to the side of the room and hands it to the first person. Now the speaker walks back to the front of the audience to continue speaking.

As the speaker talks, some of the audience is wondering where that object is, so they look to see who has it. The speaker has lost their attention. Whenever the person with the object turns around in his or her seat, noise is made. Both the movement and the noise draw attention. Now the speaker has lost the attention not only of the person passing the object and the person to whom the object is being passed but also all the other audience members whose attention has been diverted.

Whenever a speaker opts to distribute copies of a page of information, the listeners sit and read the page before the speaker is ready to explain it. When the listeners are reading, the speaker does not have their attention. There are rarely enough advantages to overcome the disadvantages of a speaker passing anything around the audience. Beginning speakers should certainly avoid the practice.

4. Showing

A speaker must talk about a visual aid while showing it, must talk to the audience (not the visual aid), and must put away the visual whenever not directly referring to it.

Though we have discussed that the appearance of an aid must be simple to understand and easy for the audience to see and though we have mentioned that the speaker must instruct the listener as to what the aid means, we have not mentioned some important factors when the actual displaying of the aid occurs.

Let's suppose you have three visual aids, one for each subdivision in the body of the speech. The temptation is to take care of the aids right away so you do not have to worry about setting them up during the speech. So you tape them to the chalkboard or prop them on easels before you begin. Then you turn around to look at the audience and begin your introduction. What do you think the audience will be doing? That's right, just what any curious onlooker would do: look at the visual aids, read them, and wonder when you are going to use them. So the speaker's strong attention-grabber has been diluted by the eye-catching visual aids. Show each visual aid **only** when you are ready to discuss it.

Likewise, if you choose to leave the first visual aid on display after you are finished with it, some of the listeners will be paying attention to it and not to you. Whenever you are finished with a visual, put the aid face down so the audience has no diversions. If you have written on the board, when you are finished referring to the information, erase it. When you are finished explaining an overhead transparency, turn off the machine until you are ready for another. Always remove any visuals when you are finished with them.

Especially important is the way in which you show an aid or perform a demonstration. Part of the time, you do need to look at the aid. But if you have rehearsed enough, you will be able to look briefly and then return your eye contact to the audience. The audience is your reason for using the aid. The audience is your primary concern, not the aid. Do not turn your back to the audience and then point to each part of the visual aid, talking to it rather than to the audience. You should know the wording well enough to say it while watching the audience. You need to have strong eye contact, and you need to gain feedback from the audience so you know whether they understand what you are saying or need further explanation.

To help you remember the four important aspects of presenting visual aids, notice that the first letter of each spells out the word "aids": appearance, instruction, distribution, and showing.

Now that we have discussed the facets of delivery and the uses of visuals, you have all the knowledge you need to become a superb speaker. All speaking presentations consist of two large categories: (1) content and (2) delivery. Both heavily influence the impression made on the audience. If either area is weak, the other area is harmed also, creating a negative overall impression.

Usually evaluation forms divide the speech into these two large categories of content and delivery. For a sample evaluation form, see Appendix A.

As a practiced musician or an athlete begins an important competition, initial nervousness may show. Shortly, however, the performer concentrates on the job at hand. The potential negatives from too much nervous energy turn into positive nervous energy in a short amount of time. What was an overabundance of nervous energy becomes extra nervous energy *under control*. The reason the nervous energy was able to be controlled and turned into an advantage (a cutting edge of performance) is because lots of rehearsals occurred before the actual performance. If very little practice had occurred before the competition, errors would occur, which would then continue to undermine self-confidence, cause additional nervous errors, and predictably end in failure.

Athletes, musicians, singers, actors, actresses, and entertainers must practice to develop and improve their skills. The more they practice, the better they become; the better they become, the more self-confidence they gain. The same is true for you, the public speaker.

The more experience you gain in informative speaking, the easier you will learn the skills of persuading an audience—our next speech goal.

Note

1. David A. Peoples, *Presentations Plus*, John Wiley, New York, 1992, p. 89.

12 Choosing a Persuasive Topic, Purpose, and Proposition

You need to have adequate knowledge about informative speaking before attempting the more difficult challenge of persuasive speaking. Once you have prepared, practiced, and delivered several information speeches, you will more easily be able to transfer to a goal of persuading someone.

First we need to define *persuasion*. Persuasion is that which attempts to shape, reinforce, or change another's beliefs and/or actions. In contrast, the informative speech attempts merely to increase the listeners' knowledge, not influence beliefs or actions. Though a persuasion speech will contain information, its main goal is to persuade. Thus, information exists only inasmuch as it is necessary to aid the persuasive goal.

Simplify Your First Attempts at Persuasion

There are vast compilations of research on persuasion. There are more books on it than it is possible to read in a lifetime. Research is still being done, and books continue to be written. For those beginning the art of persuasion, the best policy is to start simply.

Whenever I ask the students in my Persuasive Speaking course how they want to be different by the end of the quarter, many usually respond by saying they want to be able to get others to do whatever they want them to. If such a goal were possible, we would all be rich or all be president or own our own companies, etc., etc., etc. Do not think of persuasion in terms of the impossible; you will never achieve success if you do not have a clear view of your options.

First, let's look at the layers of communication that are possible:

1. *Intrapersonal* (communication with the self; that is, personal thoughts).
2. *Interpersonal* (communication with one other person).
3. *Small group* (communication with three to seven others).
4. *Public* (communication before an audience; that is, public speaking).
5. *Mass* (communication with the masses; that is, media such as newspapers, magazines, radio, and TV).

It is important for us to realize that we have long been involved in the first three types of communication: intrapersonal, interpersonal, and small group. Let's look at the first type in terms of persuasion.

In an intrapersonal relationship, only the self is involved. Each of us has constant thoughts active in the brain, but how aware are you that many of these thoughts involve persuasion of the self?

For example, whenever you debate whether or not to go to class, to apply for a job, to take a job, to date someone, to get married, to get a divorce, to have children, or to buy something, you are experiencing the intrapersonal arguments involved in persuasion. Ultimately, you will make a decision, and one side will win.

Now let's expand the internal dilemmas to reflect higher stakes. Whenever you debate whether or not to overeat, to starve yourself (anorexia), to binge and then purge (bulimia), to take another drink (drunkenness—alcoholism), to use drugs (drug addiction), to hit someone, to steal, or to cheat, you are experiencing the intrapersonal struggles of persuading yourself. Ultimately, you will perform action, and one side will win; the other side will lose.

Any time any of us have done something and then felt guilty for it or thought it was wrong, we did not persuade ourselves into doing

what we believed was best. Any time we have procrastinated study-
ing for a test, writing a report, cleaning the car, organizing our files,
or tackling any job we dislike, we fail to persuade ourselves to do what
we know we should be doing. If you and I cannot persuade ourselves
to do what we believe we should do, how do we expect to persuade
others? If persuading ourselves to do the right thing is difficult or, at
times, impossible, then we should realize persuading **someone else**
to do what we want is going to be even more difficult.

There is no quick and easy way to learn to persuade others. Nonetheless, there are some principles of persuasion that lay a foundation
for the skill of persuasive speaking. As with skills, becoming good
takes knowledge, practice, constructive criticism, and a lifetime of
experience. A person never reaches perfection, only improvement.

To begin building a foundation for persuasion as a public speaker,
the first question to ask yourself is, **How do I choose a topic?**

Choose a Topic Based on Your Interests

The first prerequisite for any speech is that you, the speaker, have
an interest in the topic. Analyze your beliefs and interests by writing
the answers to the following questions.

1. What have I heard on the news lately that upset me?
2. What have I read recently that made me angry, sad, or concerned? What
   have I read or seen that pointed out an injustice?
3. When have I debated (perhaps argued) with friends, and what was the
   topic about which we were disagreeing?
4. What usual disagreements do I have with my parents, my siblings, and
   other relatives?
5. What movies have I seen that I really got involved in, that deeply moved
   my emotions?

Your answers to these questions will help you discover what persuasive topics already interest you.

Lastly, your decision on a topic will be guided by the time limitations of your speech. If your time limit is five minutes, you do not have
time to cover a massive topic, such as what changes, if any, should be

made in the current welfare system or why the United States should intervene in the affairs of other countries. As a result, your topic must be narrowed considerably. Your topic choice is partially determined by how much time you have to use supporting details from your own research. Some topics require both extensive research and then long enough time allowance to cite some of that research. The following topic list is intended only as a guide. You should place a check beside any topic that suddenly hits you—that is, that makes you realize you feel strongly. It is "potential" for a topic, depending on other factors discussed in this chapter.

Acid Rain
AIDS
Affirmative Action
AirBag Laws
Air Pollution
Age for Drinking Alcohol
Alcohol
Alternative Education
Alternative Energy
Alternative Medicine
Animal Research or
    Experimentation
Birth Control
Bureaucracy
Capital Punishment
Capitalism
Child Abuse
Class Discrimination
Confidentiality
Credit Bureaus
Credit Cards
Criminal Rehabilitation
Criminal Rights
Date Rape
Dieting
Disciplining Children
Discrimination
Divorce Laws
Drug Tests
Drinking Laws
Drunk Driving Laws

Education System
Educational Mainstreaming
Elder Abuse
Electroshock Therapy
Endangered Species
Environment Greenhouse
    Effect
Environmental Laws
Euthanasia—The Right to Die
Family Structure
Genetic Engineering
Government Regulation
Gun Control
Health Maintenance
    Organizations
Homosexuality
Insanity Defense
Intelligence Testing
Interpersonal Relationships
Juvenile Crime
Latchkey Children
Mandatory Retirement
Medical Costs
Native Americans
News Bias
Nursing Homes
Obscenity
Organ Donation
Ozone
Pet Ownership by Children
Pesticides

Police Brutality
Police Limitations
Pornography
Poverty
Private Lives of Public Officials
Prostitution
Racism
Right to Withhold Medical
    Treatment
Seat Belt Laws
Sex Education
Sex Roles
Single Parents
Smoking Laws
Social Emphasis on Thinness
Social Security
Stereotyping
Street Crime
Surrogate Motherhood
Test-Tube Babies
Toxic Chemicals
TV Sex
TV Violence
Victim's Rights in the Justice
    System
Vitamin Consumption
Welfare System
White-Collar Crime
Wife Abuse
Women's Rights
Working Mothers

Choose a Topic Based on Your Audience

As with any speech topic, it is important not only that you be interested in the topic but also that your audience be interested. Of the topics you are interested in, which ones do you think will interest your audience? Part of your decision about the interests of the audience will be based on an analysis of the listeners similar to that discussed in Chapter 2.

The most important question to answer about an audience that you want to persuade is, How do they feel about your topic? Placed on a continuum, you might want to dissect your listeners according to the following scale:

Number of Listeners:

Strongly Agree	_____	Agree	_____
Disagree	_____	Strongly Disagree	_____
Neutral	_____	Apathetic	_____

The way the audience members fit into these categories will determine what appeals will work best with them. A neutral audience is one that may have some facts on both sides of the issue but has not yet decided on a stand. It does not necessarily mean the audience has no interest in the topic.

In contrast, the definition of *Apathetic*, the last item on the list, is "having no feeling, emotion, or interest; indifferent, unconcerned." It is last on the list because it is often considered the most difficult audience to persuade. An audience that strongly opposes some idea at least is interested in the topic, but an audience that doesn't care at all also doesn't care which side you take. They are least likely to listen to anything about the topic and do not want information on either side.

Though the tendency of beginning speakers is to believe that the least desirable audience is one that stands on the opposite side, the most difficult is one with the attitude of "What do I care?"

When you have decided a topic interests both you and your audience and have analyzed the listeners according to their agreement or disagreement, you are ready to decide your persuasive aim; that is, what you want **from** the listener. In other words, what do you want to accomplish?

Do You Want to Reinforce Your Listeners' Beliefs?

One of three possibilities in persuading others is realizing they hold the same beliefs or values as you and then aiming the speech at **reinforcing** their already existent beliefs. Do not mistake this with informing. Your purpose here is to make their belief stronger, to make them more certain than ever that they have chosen the "correct" side.

For example, a minister or priest or rabbi believes in the particular religion he or she represents. When talking to the congregation of believers each week, the goal is to reinforce those beliefs. Similarly, a speaker at a Republican or a Democratic convention speaks to masses of individuals who already are Republicans or Democrats. At such a convention, many of the speeches are to further their current platforms and strengthen the beliefs of the group.

Do You Want to Change Your Listeners' Beliefs?

If you do not want merely to reinforce already existent beliefs, then you likely want to **change** those beliefs to match yours. It is usually easier to convince an audience that is undecided than to convince one that is opposed to what you say. Furthermore, you must discover how many in the audience disagree with you, how deeply they hold their convictions, and why they believe as they do. This information allows you to analyze the best strategies to use.

For example, if you want to change someone's religion, you can assume you have an extremely difficult (perhaps impossible) task ahead. Analyzing the audience can make a difference in your tactics. Discovering that some members in the audience are wavering about their religious beliefs would result in using one type of strategy, while discovering that an entire audience has deep convictions about their religion would result in a different strategy—or perhaps better, a different topic. A speaker needs to be realistic about what can and cannot be accomplished in **one** public speech!

Do You Want to Move Your Audience to Action?

As we progress to the third persuasive aim, your task becomes progressively more difficult. The most difficult type of persuasion is that which attempts to get others to act physically. That is, you may want them to vote for you, to buy something from you, to write their legislators, to fill out a form, to attend an important meeting, to sign a petition—but always this type of purpose wants the listener to act physically. Because action takes time and effort beyond merely agreeing with someone, the listener is less likely to fulfill your wishes and be persuaded by you.

The simpler you can make the task, the more likely you are to get some people to act on it.

For example, if you want your audience to write their legislators and thus provide them with representatives' names and addresses on a poster, overhead, or chalkboard, most will not bother copying the information, let alone going to the effort of writing a letter and mailing it.

It would be a little better if, after the speech, you distributed a list of legislators' names and addresses; then you know that each listener has a copy, but then again, most of your listeners will lay the sheet aside and forget about it. It still takes too much time and effort to write a letter, find an envelope, and stamp and mail it.

You would vastly improve the odds of getting your listeners to act if you had written a petition or letter and had it available for signatures. In this case, you have already done the work, and all the audience needs to do is sign their names. You will even do the mailing!

The easier you make a task for your audience, the more likely you are to move them to action.

Likewise, asking people who previously haven't voted to vote for a certain issue may not get them to the voting booth at all. Increase your chances by simplifying the process. Show them the ballot, explain the wording, and then show them how to mark it. Tell the group where they will be voting and have a map of directions to distribute. Furthermore, you might indicate what hours tend to have the fewest people voting, so they can get in and out quickly. Discovering why these people haven't voted before is the key to knowing how to appeal to them. When you supply viable solutions to help solve **their** problems and make simple what you want done, you will improve your chances of success.

The more you can show the audience how they will benefit, the more likely the audience will be persuaded to act. Magazines use this tactic when trying to gain new subscribers. Several of them indicate not only what the content of the magazine is but also what they will send to a subscriber (camera, sport bag, radio, watch, etc.). If you can convince the audience they will gain enough from performing the action you want them to, they will be activated.

The goal of reinforcing an audience is considered the easiest, with convincing an audience next in difficulty; activating is unquestionably the most difficult, and the persuader must rely on the techniques of the first two in order to move an audience to action.

Deciding whether your aim is to reinforce existing values, change current beliefs, or motivate to action is important because this knowledge guides you to word your persuasive speech purpose in one of three ways: proposition of fact, proposition of value, or proposition of policy.

Understand How to Word a Proposition of Fact

A *fact* is defined as "a verified statement" or "an assertion having an objective reality," so how can we be persuasive if something is a fact?

The answer is because some facts are not so easily "verified." If I assert that marijuana is a drug, there is little problem with realizing the truth of the statement.

But let's say I say that marijuana is legal under some conditions. I may now be making a statement that you cannot verify so easily. In fact, someone next to me may say, "No, it isn't. It's a Federal law that anyone caught with marijuana has possession of an illegal substance and can be prosecuted." Someone else says, "Making marijuana legal under a doctor's prescription is under discussion by lawmakers," but someone else contradicts and replies, "No, it isn't; that was a rumor." That means the current FACT is that marijuana may be legal under some conditions; it may be illegal under any conditions; it may be under discussion by lawmakers—or it may not be.

So a problem is that though facts may have an objective reality, we may not be privy to that reality when we do not have enough knowledge.

Furthermore, facts may differ according to how, when, and by whom they were established. Let's look at a topic that will demonstrate this point.

What facts might we want to know about the topic of teenage pregnancies?

1. How many are there?
2. How many mothers remain single?
3. How many get married?
4. How many want the baby?
5. What problems will they encounter?
6. What is the average income of the family?

First of all, please notice that propositions of fact use wording that indicates something is or is not true. For example, suppose someone says, "Over one million American teenage girls get pregnant each year." That is a statement of fact, but whenever such a fact is given, the ethical speaker must supply the source. Even with a source supplied, however, certain questions may be asked by members of a discerning audience. For example, what is the age of the various pregnant teens? A pregnant teenager who is thirteen years old and one who is nineteen may have vastly different implications. Yet both are teens. Another question should be how the survey was taken. Were some hospitals asked to supply statistics and then a formula used to calculate the total number? Did the survey cover the East Coast, West Coast, Southern United States, Northern United States, and the Midwest? Or did it use only one or two areas and calculate the rest?

In other words, facts may vary based on how carefully a survey was run, on who performed the survey (the group may bias the results), and on when the survey was run. Statistics change from year to year, from decade to decade, and from century to century.

Once facts are gathered on a topic, the thesis asserts those facts as true and attempts to prove them by citing experts, research, case studies, and statistics as proof of the main ideas. Below is wording for a sample thesis.

THESIS WORDING FOR A PROPOSITION OF FACT

1. More U.S. teenagers than ever before are becoming pregnant, giving birth out of wedlock, and needing welfare assistance.

2. More teenage males than ever before are demonstrating irresponsibility by refusing to marry the mother of their children and refusing to give financial support to their family.

Notice that these statements of "facts" need to be verified through citing statistics from various experts, such as doctors, psychologists, sociologists, U.S. government surveys, welfare office statistics, and so forth. The more reliable the sources, the more likely the audience will believe the information.

So you can see that facts are not so easily verifiable sometimes, and it is often through our subjective interpretation of various facts that we form our opinions about a topic. These opinions are the basis of our personal value system, which provides the source of all propositions of value.

Understand How to Word a Proposition of Value

A proposition of value reflects the speaker's personal ethical system by asserting an opinion using words of value: "beneficial or harmful," "best or worst," "fair or unfair," "right or wrong," "just or unjust," "good or bad," "positive or negative," "safe or dangerous," "wise or foolish," "ethical or unethical," "advantageous or problematic," and so forth. These words are from a personal value system, and a persuasive speech using them has as its purpose agreement from the audience.

For example, if we take the idea of teen pregnancies, which we used to demonstrate the wording for a proposition of fact, and turn the speech purpose into a proposition of value, we might use the following wording.

THESIS WORDING FOR A PROPOSITION OF VALUE

1. Teenage pregnancies are **harming** (value word) society because the young mothers-to-be become school dropouts, mere children are

inadequately (value word) raising babies, and unmarried teen mothers **unfairly** (value word) tax the welfare system.

2. Pregnant teenagers are **victimized** by society because they are **deprived** of an education, denied financial support by **irresponsible** fathers, and disproportionately **burdened** by societal stigma.

Notice how the wording is not that something is or is not true but rather that something is "bad"; that is, in these cases, the value words are all negative.

In a proposition of value, to reinforce the beliefs of audience members who already agree or to convince those who do not agree, a speaker needs to rely on some propositions of fact as support for the thesis. Reliable and recent research supporting the value statements must be cited. In other words, a proposition of value relies on facts for evidence.

Understand How to Word a Proposition of Policy

If the speaker's aim is to move the audience to action, he or she uses action words preceded by "should" or "should not" or by "must" or "must not." An action word is whatever the speaker wants the audience to physically do.

Some typical action statements bombarding the public are "You should vote for me because . . . ," "You must buy (name of a product) because . . . ," "You should (or should not) use drugs because . . . ," "Growers should (or should not) spray chemicals on plants because . . . ," and "You must vote yes on Issue 4 because . . . ."

How might we turn our teenage pregnancy thesis from the proposition of fact or of value into a proposition of policy?

THESIS WORDING FOR A PROPOSITION OF POLICY

The government **should** (or "should not") **provide** education, work programs, and child care for teenage mothers.

The proposition of policy is considered the most complicated of the persuasive purposes because it contains underlayments of both a proposition of value and a proposition of fact. It is also the most difficult if its intent is not merely to gain agreement but also to move to action.

To understand these propositions, look at the following layers we typically hear in this society.

1. Politician

    Policy: You should vote for me
    Value: Because I am good or fair or just or honest
    Fact: Because I will lower taxes, decrease crime, increase jobs

2. Clothing Clerk

    Policy: Honey, you should buy that outfit
    Value: Because you look so good, attractive, slender
    Fact: Because the vertical lines are slenderizing and the color matches your eyes.

3. Car Salesperson

    Policy: You should buy this car
    Value: Because it's a good car, the best on the market
    Fact: Because it gets 25 m.p.g., it has rust-proofing, and it has an extended warranty.

The proposition of policy is often a statement seeking action, not just reinforcement or agreement. Therefore, to move the audience to action, the speaker uses propositions of value to gain agreement about the rightness of the action and then propositions of fact to support the value system.

Now that you know the difference in wording of the various propositions, you need to learn to organize your speech. In the next chapter, we will look at one of the most popular outlines used for persuasive speaking and see how it is similar to and different from what you've already learned. In addition we will learn about supporting and delivering a persuasive presentation.

"HE STUDIED PERSUASION AND MOTIVATIONAL APPEALS."

13 Organizing, Supporting, and Delivering a Persuasive Speech

There are certainly similarities in the organization of either an informative or a persuasive speech. The differences, however, center around what you want from your audience. From an informational presentation, you want them to walk away understanding and remembering your main ideas. From a persuasive presentation, you want to influence your listeners' beliefs. Though both presentations should be interesting, they differ somewhat in the motivational use of supporting details.

The Motivated Sequence Uses Five Steps

The motivated sequence is so attributed to Alan Monroe that it is often called Monroe's motivated sequence.[1] This organization uses a psychological approach based on a specific ordering of steps to motivate an audience. Table 13.1 shows the steps to Monroe's well-known formula (on the left-hand side); on the right-hand side are the steps you learned from the "Organizational Outline" at the end of Chapter 9. Notice how they parallel one another in the function each step is to perform.

Table 13.1 The Motivated Sequence and the Standard Outline

Motivated Sequence:	Standard Outline:
Attention (Grab audience attention)	Intro's Attention-Grabber
Need (Show a problem and relate to audience's lives)	Intro's Relevance Statement
Satisfaction (Present a solution)	Intro's Thesis Statement
Visualization (Paint a detailed picture to help audience visualize solution working)	Body of Speech with supporting details
Action (Speech ends with a call to action)	Conclusion

Below is a sample of a speech on drug testing, aligned with the above outline headings.

SAMPLE SPEECH ON DRUG TESTING FOLLOWING FIVE-STEP OUTLINE

Attention:

Had you been in New York City on August 28, 1991, and had you decided to ride the subway, you might have experienced the subway crash that occurred that day. Five people were killed; 171 were injured. The cause of the crash? A drunken motorman. In addition, authorities found traces of cocaine in the motorman's cab.

In January 1988, a commuter transport crashed near Durango, Colorado, killing nine people. The cause of this crash? The pilot's use of cocaine.

Need/Relevance:

Likely you and I and our loved ones periodically or regularly depend on public transportation: a plane, a bus, a taxi, or a train. And when we climb aboard whatever mode of transport we have chosen, we assume that we are in the hands of someone who is competent. But as you can see, that might be a false assumption. In fact, we may be in grave danger because our pilot, our driver, or our motorman may be abusing alcohol and other drugs. To protect those who depend on public transportation, drug testing of those responsible for our safety is a necessity.

But drug testing is not without its problems. Some of you may have experienced at your work place the humiliation that comes from having someone watch while you urinate into a cup to be sure no switching takes place. Furthermore, drug testing can give false positives, as well as be influenced by legally prescribed drugs and even some foods. And on top of these problems, there is the high cost of laboratory testing. These are legitimate complaints about drug testing, and I would like to address these issues and make some suggestions that might help all of us find a solution.

Satisfaction Step/Thesis Statement:

Drug testing of public transportation employees responsible for our safety will be beneficial to all involved if the tests are both accurate and cost-effective.

Visualization/Body:

First of all, drug testing of public transportation employees can be performed so that the tests are accurate. Both the FDA and the American Medical Association guidelines suggest ways to decrease inaccuracies, thereby increasing accuracy. These suggestions are available to companies doing the testing and employees who are being tested. Within these guidelines is a listing of foods that can give a false reading as well as legal drugs that may affect the results. By following guidelines and informing the employer of legitimate exceptions in advance, those being tested will not be victims of false readings and the resultant humiliation from inaccuracy. In a recent issue of the magazine *The Economist,* in order to maintain objectivity in testing so that test results cannot be skewed by bosses who might be biased, IBM hires outside, independent firms to provide lab results. Furthermore, all drug-positive tests are double-checked by confirmation tests and are visibly marked as such so that the lab technicians take extra precautions in the double-testing process. Since the occurrences of inaccuracies from the beginnings of drug testing, special efforts have been made to remedy the problem. As a result, accurate and fair drug testing of those responsible for our safe public transportation is now more certain than in the past.

Not only can drug testing for employees be accurate, but also it can be cost effective. Of course, expense is often mentioned as a problem of the testing. But what about the cost of errors by those employees who abuse drugs? According to an article in *The Economist*, drug abuse costs businesses from thirty-three to one-hundred billion dollars each year. Surely, the cost of a ruined public transportation vehicle, the increase in insurance rates to the company responsible for the accident, the company's cost in legal fees, and the cost incurred by lawsuits would be nonexistent if accurate drug testing were enforced. Furthermore, the cost to a company in getting a bad public image costs the company in future customers as well as negates the money spent on past positive advertising. And, most importantly, we cannot put a monetary value on your life, my life, or the life of a loved one. Should we have to worry about our safety when we use public transportation? Don't we expect the engine to be checked, enough fuel to be provided, train tracks to be working, plane wings to be de-iced, brakes to be working? Why shouldn't we also have safety checks of the operator of the vehicle? What good is a perfectly safe vehicle and an unsafe operator? When determining cost, one of the prices isn't monetary and material but rather emotional and physical. In fact, a report by the U.S. Chamber of Commerce claims that employees who use drugs are three times more likely to produce injury than those who don't. On December 12, 1992, CBS News indicated that the government recommended random testing for alcohol abuse by public transportation operators, estimating at least 1,200 lives would be saved over a decade. Whatever the cost of drug testing, surely it is worth the price of human lives.

Action Step/Conclusion:

Admittedly there have been problems with drug testing, and these difficulties have caused many to claim that it should not be done. But instead of deciding the testing itself is bad, I'd like you to think about working to solve the problems surrounding poor testing so we can ensure it is accurate and fair to the employee, cost effective for the employer, and safe for all who rely on public transportation. I hope you are aware that I have not advocated testing for all employees in all types of jobs. The concern I have involves only public transportation. The next time you step onto a bus, board a plane, climb into a train, or hail a taxi, I hope you remember what I've said today. And as you ride to your destination, think about the potential for the operator to be drunk (as on the New York City subway) or to be high on drugs (as in the Colorado plane crash). Then think about the security of knowing he or she has tested negative for drug use.

Use Reasoning to Help Support Persuasive Speeches

Using reasoning to support your claims means to "critically examine, seeking out inferences or conclusions from evidence given." Basically there are three types of reasoning: deductive, inductive, and causal.

1. Deductive Reasoning

Deductive reasoning starts with a generalization and then supports it with details. The general statement is an assumption, which the facts support by "deducing" logically a direct correlation between the generalization and then the facts which follow it. Examples of deductive reasoning are shown below.

DEDUCTIVE REASONING

a. Generalization: Guns are potentially dangerous weapons.
   Detail: Jane owns a gun as a weapon.
   Deduction: Jane is potentially dangerous.
b. Generalization: People who own guns but do not know how to use them can be dangerous to themselves.
   Detail #1:   Jane owns a gun.
   Detail #2:   Jane does not know how to use a gun.
   Deduction: Jane could be dangerous to herself.

One danger with deductive reasoning is that the generalization may be contestable. Analyze it to see if it is faulty. For example, look at the following:

c. Generalization: People who own guns are dangerous.
   Detail: Connie owns a gun.
   Deduction: Connie is dangerous.

Though the deduction above is correct when based on the previous statements, the generalization itself is faulty. You must critically analyze the truthfulness of any generalizations you use when applying

deductive reasoning. Often, generalizations that use words like *all,*
everyone, always, never, and *no one* are called sweeping generalizations
and are too broad to be correct. Beware of such inclusive words.

2. Inductive Reasoning

Inductive reasoning lists a series of details and arrives at a conclusion. Hence, it is the opposite order of deductive reasoning. Examples
of inductive reasoning are listed below.

INDUCTIVE REASONING

Detail #1: Your neighbor across the street walks to her mailbox,
opens it, and pulls out some mail.

Detail #2: Your neighbor on the west walks to his mailbox,
opens it, and pulls out some mail

Induction: The mail has been delivered for the day, and there is
likely mail in your mailbox.

Notice with inductive reasoning that you must be careful of your
conclusion; it is an assumption based on some facts that **seem** to point
to the generalization. It would be possible that the facts are deceiving.
For example, perhaps the two neighbors did not get their previous
day's mail. Hence, the current day's mail might not have come at all.
The more details you have, the stronger your conclusion. Beware of
jumping to conclusions, though, and of sweeping generalizations
such as we saw with deductive reasoning.

An example of too broad a generalization follows.

Detail #1: In a grocery in Podunk, I got shortchanged when I
bought a soft drink.

Detail #2: When I got gas for my car in Podunk, the gas atten-
dant started to charge me too much.

Induction: All the people in Podunk are cheats.

In fact, not only are all the people in Podunk likely not cheats, but even
the two errors that were made may not have been done on purpose or

by cheats either. There is not enough evidence to reach a conclusion until further research is done; that is, until further facts and details are listed.

3. Causal Reasoning

Causal reasoning makes the assumption that one event causes a second event. It establishes a direct correlation: If the one is present, then so is the other. This type of reasoning can be very tricky because two events may occur together, but one may not actually cause the other. Look at the examples listed below.

CAUSE AND EFFECT REASONING

Detail #1:   Ice cream sales increase in the summer.
Detail #2:   Incidence of theft increases in the summer.

Incorrect Cause and Effect Assumption: The consumption of ice
    cream causes an increase in theft.

There is not enough evidence here to make a cause and effect relationship. Other causes might contribute to the effect. Perhaps people keep their windows open in the summer, making entry by thieves easier. People with children tend to plan vacations in the summer, leaving their houses empty. Perhaps it is easier for thieves to commit crimes in warm weather, unencumbered by layers of extra clothing. Even these assumptions must be tested to prove whether there is a cause and effect correlation. The questions to ask here are, Does the proposed cause have the same effect each time, and, furthermore, Is the effect absent when the proposed cause is also absent?

This type of reasoning is the most difficult because it is easy to make a cause and effect assumption that is not true.

Though you will sometimes use deductive, inductive, and causal reasoning, as beginners you will more likely notice other experts using it as you research. You need more than your own use of reasoning to support claims about your topic; to persuade an audience, you need to do library research such as is indicated in Chapter 5.

Cite Research to Support Your Claims

To support each of your claims, you must use ideas from experts, describe relevant case studies from professional documents, and cite figures from research. But one of the difficulties for the speaker is knowing how much to say about the source.

When you use research to support your claims, remember one major rule: **YOU MUST TELL THE AUDIENCE THE SOURCE OF YOUR INFORMATION.** The minimum you should indicate about your source is the author's name and professional title. Depending on your topic, you may need to provide the year the research was done. For example, if you cite the number of traffic deaths each year, when the research was done makes a big difference, since these statistics change yearly. Likewise, if you claim the rate of a certain type of cancer is increasing, you need to cite some previous years' figures and then some current years'. Frequently, it adds to your credibility to indicate the name of the magazine or the book. For example, if you are quoting a doctor and indicate the research came from a current year's issue of the *Journal of the American Medical Association,* your claims are strengthened by citing such a strong source. **(Warning:** You should be aware that even though something is published, it may not be true.) The more expert sources you have, the more believable your claims will be.

Tie your sources together by using some of your own ideas and words and by repeating the respective subdivision of the thesis—in other words, by using those transitional hooks discussed in Chapter 8. The details in the body of the speech are to support your main ideas and add expert support to your side of the topic. Your main ideas are not a listing of what others believe; your main ideas are what you want the audience to believe or do, with the supporting details and citations of experts supporting your own beliefs.

1. Use Quotations Correctly. Concerning quoting someone, it is often best to put most of the quotation in your own wording because audiences tend to get bored by the reading of long quotations or the bad habit of the speaker reading several in a row without transitions between them and without relating them to the topic idea. In Chapter 7 under the heading "Using Details Makes A Subdivision Interesting And Memorable," you can reread the subdivision on stress and note the transitions and the way the sources are cited. Notice that they have transitions between them as reminders for the audience each time of what the case study is proving.

2. Use Statistics in Limited Quantity. It is good practice to use some statistics or figures, but to cite several in a row is a bad practice—especially without a visual aid. An audience cannot remember sequences of numbers; often they cannot remember even one! Use only those that are vital in supporting your claims. If using even five figures or statistics, you should have a chart that you explain to help simplify those figures and aid the audience in understanding. Also, numbers should always be rounded off; it is much easier to remember "almost 4,000 cases" than it is to remember "3,898 cases." Always round off to the nearest whole number. In the above, notice that we did not round it off to "3,900 cases." The simpler you make a figure, the easier it is to comprehend it.

3. Use Analogies With Large Numbers. If you use large numbers (such as hundreds of thousands, millions, billions, or trillions), you need to relate it to something that the audience can comprehend.

For example, let's assume you are comparing Japan to the United States. At one point in your speech, you indicate that Japan consists of 143,759 square miles and Alaska, 570,830 square miles. Rounding off these figures is not enough to give the audience any meaning. Likewise, rounding off Japan's population to 120,000,000 and Alaska's to 402,000 has little meaning for the audience. It hardly has much meaning to you as a reader, and you can see the figures! But if you were to say that Alaska is big enough that four Japans would fit inside its space, you give a picture to your audience, a comparison they can comprehend. Likewise, if you were to say, "Though the country of Japan is one fourth the size of America's largest state, Japan has 300 times the population of Alaska." Or perhaps you would say, "Though the state of California and the country of Japan are close in size, Japan squeezes into its boundaries five times the population of California." Somehow you need to offer your audience a comparison they can understand. Figures alone are seldom remembered or understood. Furthermore, if your material is difficult, decrease the rate of your delivery so the audience has time to understand your points.

4. Represent Your Sources Honestly. Be sure that you represent your sources as they intended. That is, you are bound by speaker ethics never to misrepresent which side your source supports on the topic. You are morally obligated to use figures and statistics as the authors or researchers intended them to be used. Never change them in such a way that you create a different meaning from the original intent, and never make up any figures on your own.

Appeal Psychologically to Your Audience

Besides citing experts and research, another method of support within the body of the speech is for you to use psychological appeals. These can be interwoven with the support from various experts, research, and case studies. These appeals are effective because they tap into a hierarchy of human needs first introduced by Maslow that psychologists have long identified as basic to all humans.[2] Some of the most common needs for use by the persuader are listed below and are based on a listing by Dr. Charles Whitfield.[3]

1. Safety

Though we need food, clothing, and shelter, we also want to avoid accidents, fires, violence, and other risks involving us and our loved ones. Anyone showing us how to accomplish this better will have our attention. Speech topics on fire extinguishers or home burglar alarms play on the psychological desire for safety.

2. Acceptance

We gain some identity from socializing with others. If we believe others feel positive toward us, we tend to feel positive about ourselves. Advertising heavily plays on the need for acceptance when it advertises mouthwashes, breath mints, and deodorants. Speakers appeal to this by showing advantages of being a part of a group, such as volunteer organizations, political parties, or social clubs.

3. Accomplishment/Power

Many of us already have food, shelter, and clothing. Yet we want special foods, huge houses with three-car garages, and more clothing than we need. Wealth is a goal of many, many Americans, and we will listen to those who can tell us how we can gain the material items we want. The credit-card industry has succeeded in getting our business based on our desire for material goods. Speeches on how to get a better job, make more money, or have smarter investments involve this appeal.

4. Participation

Some organizations can make us feel virtuous for giving without getting anything in return. United Way is an organization aiming at our altruistic nature. *Altruism* means "generosity without self-gain." Hospitals, heart funds, and cancer research centers seek donations using this psychological appeal of altruism, of participating out of the "goodness of one's heart." A persuasive speaker who can make an audience feel good about being part of a cause, even though there is nothing material to be gained, will be successful. A speech on getting listeners to volunteer time or money for a "good cause" appeals to our desire to participate.

5. Being Real

The psychological appeal of being real involves not only our love of what is natural in our environment but also our desire to look "naturally" attractive. Some states produce ads for vacation spots by showing waterfalls, mountains, forests—untouched by industrialization. Indeed, a speaker who appeals to us to conserve our environment is appealing to our love of nature (and our safety). Many commercials for makeup indicate that wearing it will make a woman look "naturally" beautiful. Also, many lotions, shampoos, and cream rinses use large colorful print to indicate natural ingredients, such as aloe, lanolin, natural apple pectin, vitamins, and herbs.

6. Sexuality

The human need and desire for sexuality is played upon by cologne names (Ambush, Passion, Interlude, Taboo, Opium), clothing displays, and even car ads. One of my favorite automobile ads, which I saved some years ago, is a full-page ad with a picture of a car and three words in huge type: SEX, POWER, AND 25 MPG!

These six major appeals can be valuable aids in persuading an audience. More than one can be used in a speech, depending on the topic, but it is important to remember to use these appeals ethically, logically, and with valid supporting details from a variety of reputable sources.

Build Credibility in the Introduction

Credibility is defined as "the quality of inspiring belief, of being viewed as trustworthy." No matter what the topic, a speaker must be viewed as credible for the audience to be willing to listen and to consider the speaker's views.

The introduction of a persuasive speech will fulfill all the functions discussed in Chapter 9, but will have additional emphasis on building credibility and will therefore be longer. Gaining this credibility is not an easy task, but the process begins in the introduction and is influenced by your attitude about yourself, your topic, and your audience. Credibility is vital in a persuasive speaking situation if it is to achieve any level of success.

1. Exhibit Self-Confidence

Your view of yourself comes through nonverbal delivery as well as the content of the speech. In other words, it is not just a matter of what you say but also of how you say it and how you act. If you believe strongly in what you say, have thoroughly researched your topic, and have rehearsed adequately, your self-confidence will show as a result. You must display confidence in order to gain it. You must be in control of yourself in order to have some influence on others.

To show you are competent, you must show control of your delivery from the introduction to the conclusion. Look directly at the eyes of various audience members. Let them know you care about them enough to look at them. Let your feelings about the topic show through your vocal variety and through your appropriate pauses. Use gestures that you feel natural using, and pause where the material might be difficult for the audience to understand. In other words, follow the good delivery practices discussed in Chapter 10.

In contrast, if you have not adequately practiced, your insecurity in the delivery will be apparent, and your trustworthiness will suffer. The introduction is the place to begin creating credibility.

2. Display Open-Mindedness

In the introduction, it is important to show the audience that you have some beliefs in common with them, especially about the topic at hand and especially if some of the listeners disagree with you. Furthermore, it is important to show that you know both sides of the issue even though you will be speaking on only one. This gives the audience confidence in your integrity and helps them perceive you as trustworthy. The difference between the introduction of a persuasive speech and that of an informative one is that a persuasive speaker must show he or she understands the opposing view and sympathizes with it. Otherwise, the opponents will immediately turn off listening by thinking of all their own counterarguments. If the speaker shows a clear knowledge of those arguments and indicates they have merit, the audience will not need to think of the opposite arguments and will appreciate the speaker's objectivity on the issue.

You cannot expect your opponents to be willing to see the advantages of your side if you are not willing to do the same with their side. You must show open-mindedness in order to have any chance of receiving the same.

3. Demonstrate Competence

Competence is demonstrated through your knowledge of the topic. You gain knowledge through your own experiences and through research. Both are valuable resources for supporting your side of the issue. Personal details interspersed with other case studies from your reading provide interest and acceptance from your audience. Furthermore, if you have training and experience in the topic area, you increase the listeners' perception of your competence and, therefore, your trustworthiness. The audience should be told of your training or experience in the introduction, though you should be sure to introduce this information in a factual, non-arrogant way. Someone who is perceived as arrogant or a braggart is disliked and frequently mistrusted.

It should be evident by now that credibility is a necessary aspect of the art of persuasion. Credibility derives from your view of yourself, your consideration of the audience's point of view, your research about the topic, and your willingness to organize and rehearse in advance of the presentation. All these factors result in the audience's judgment of your credibility as high or low.

Make Your Conclusion Brief and Powerful

The conclusion for a persuasive speech is similar to an informative speech in that it should fulfill the functions indicated in Chapter 9, but the persuasive speech must also make an appeal to the audience based on whether the speaker wants to reinforce, change, or actuate the listeners.

Remember our acronym **END** for the purposes of a speech conclusion: End with finality; name again the subdivisions of the thesis; denote power in the last sentence.

In a persuasive speech, in that powerful last sentence, you will want to appeal to the audience to agree or to act, depending on what you want from your audience. "To appeal" actually means "to arouse a sympathetic response." So you need to indicate to them whatever response you desire from them. If you intend to perform the action you desire from them, tell them that you are going to do it and when. In addition, if you can make the action seem simple for them, do it here. Show them a petition that they can sign, distribute a map, and so forth, as discussed earlier in this chapter. Anything that will make the action easier for them will further encourage them to perform the action.

Persuading an audience is a difficult goal. The difficulty does not necessarily increase with an increase in the number of listeners. We can have a difficult time when we have no external audience at all; for example, when we attempt to persuade ourselves to do something we do not want to do. Likewise, we often fail to achieve our persuasive goal when only one person is our audience; for example, a person with whom we have frequent disagreements on various issues. Convincing that one person to agree with us is as feasible as that person convincing us to agree with him or her. And so it is with larger audiences. The difficulty in persuading is always present and always requires the accomplishment of certain preliminaries as a foundation. This chapter has given that basic foundation as a starting point for you to begin learning the skill. Repeatedly practicing the steps you have learned will improve your skill. Below is a summation of those steps.

BASIC STEPS FOR A PERSUASIVE SPEECH

1. Select an interesting topic.
2. Analyze the audience.
3. Decide on a persuasive aim.
4. Correctly word the proposition.
5. Clearly organize the content.
6. Use reasoning and cite research.
7. Appeal to audience needs.
8. Create speaker credibility.
9. End with a powerful appeal.
10. Rehearse, rehearse, rehearse.

An old adage says that luck is when opportunity meets preparation. I would suggest a corollary in terms of your success in persuading. The opportunity is ever present; your success is determined by whether or not you have adequately prepared.

Having a knowledge of speech preparation is helpful for one goal: creating a public speaker. Since people spend most of their time listening, not speaking, the skill of listening is as important to the communication process as the skill of speaking. The speaker not only needs to be a good speaker but also a good listener. Knowledge of the communication cycle helps a speaker understand his or her listeners and adjust to their needs. The next chapter will help you understand the process of communication.

Notes

1. Douglas Ehninger, Bruce E. Gronbeck, and Alan H. Monroe, *Principles of Speech Communication,* 9th brief ed., Scott, Foresman, Glenview, IL, 1984, pp. 250-259.

2. Abraham Maslow, *Motivation and Personality,* Harper & Row, New York, 1970, pp. 35-58.

3. Charles L. Whitfield, M.D., *Healing The Child Within,* Health Communications, Deerfield Beach, FL, 1989, p. 18.

14 Understanding the Communication Process

So far we have discussed the steps necessary to prepare and deliver a speech. After all, **speaking** is what we are learning about, isn't it? If I walked into an empty lecture hall and delivered a speech, wouldn't I be a speaker? Though your first impulse will likely be to answer yes, do not be too hasty in your reply.

According to some definitions of *speaking* (for example, "one who speaks in public," or "one who addresses *an audience*"), I would not be a speaker. The premise behind the act of speaking is that a person wants to get an idea **across to someone else.** A speaker speaks in order to communicate, and communication implies an interchange has taken place. Hence, at least one listener must be present for the possibility of an exchange.

When I teach a college class of speech, I usually have a minimum of 25 nervous beginners. With either a quarter or semester system, that means a maximum of five speeches if I take some days to deliver lectures. When I ask my students on the first day what is on their minds concerning this course, 100 percent indicate that their speaking performance is foremost in their minds. This is certainly a logical response, since most people fear speaking in public and since most courses are titled "Effective Speaking," "Public Speaking," or "Speech 101."

Let's look at how such a title can be misleading. If each speaker delivers five speeches between five and ten minutes in length, the maximum cumulative time that any individual will speak is fifty minutes, the time slot of **ONE** day's class period. If the school is on the quarter system, that would equal one day out of thirty sessions, one thirtieth of the total time spent in class. Ninety-seven percent of the time would be spent as a member of an audience, and only 3 percent as a speaker. In a semester system, the total time spent speaking would equal one day out of forty-five sessions; 98 percent of the time would be spent as a listener, and only 2 percent as a speaker.

Yet no students ever say that foremost on their minds is becoming an effective listener. Nonetheless, most of a person's time in life, including in a speech class, is spent being a listener, not a speaker. This vital part of the communication event is often ignored. When we think about communicating, we most often think about what we are going to say, not how well we are going to listen.

In a public speaking situation, communication cannot take place without an effective listener; it can, however, take place without a very good speaker. We need, therefore, to look at ourselves not only as speakers but also as listeners. Then we can gain an awareness of the cost of poor listening.

Listening Poorly Can Be Financially Costly

An engineering friend of mine who traveled internationally to work on projects told me that in one incident of poor listening, she cost her company $100,000. Such an example may seem extreme, but each year companies indicate that poor listening adds up to tremendous monetary losses. First of all, the person who did the job incorrectly was paid to do the work and used materials at company expense. Afterward, someone has to be paid to undo the error that has been made, and the used materials often have to be discarded and new ones again provided.

Suppose, for example, that each employee of the Procter & Gamble Company made a mere $15 listening error in a year. That sounds like the company doesn't have much of a problem. But the company employs 89,000; thus, the total for the year's listening errors would be more than a million dollars.

In their study of listening training in *Fortune* 500 corporations, Andrew Wolvin and Carolyn Coakley conclude that colleges need to provide training in listening skills so the students entering the workforce will be competent listeners.[1]

Obviously, poor listening is a problem and can be quite costly—not only to companies but also to consumers; eventually, the cost incurred by poor listening is passed on to the consumer in the price of goods.

Listening Poorly Can Be Emotionally Painful

The most consistent reactions I receive from students are a result of a question I ask about listening. I want to ask you the same one.

Here's the situation: Think about a time you have been talking with someone you know quite well on an interpersonal level. Now, recall a time when you were pouring out your heart to this person, telling him or her your innermost thoughts, secrets, fears, and desires. What if that person had yawned and looked at his or her watch while you were in the middle of this story? How would you feel?

Interestingly, the response I get from some of the audience is one of recognition, indicating they have been in a similar situation and have experienced someone who has not cared enough to listen. Their reaction to the incident is that their feelings were hurt, that they stopped telling their inner feelings to the person, and that they would be cautious whenever they again decided to tell their feelings to anyone else.

Halfhearted listening is not uncommon. Since it takes two to communicate, if either the speaker or the listener stops trying, there is no communication. Either the speaker stops talking or the listener stops listening, or a combination of both. The 50 percent divorce rate might be an indicator of problems with interpersonal communication skills. If we cannot listen well to the person we are supposed to be closest to, how well do we listen to less significant others—friends, family, colleagues, and business associates?

The reasons for this difficulty in listening involve two problem areas: false assumptions about listening and lack of awareness about listening skills.

Analyze Any Assumptions You Have About Being a Good Listener

Many people unknowingly have the misconception that listening is a simple, easy, automatic process.

When you get up in the morning, many of you awake to a radio alarm. But do you remember what was being said? Do you remember all the songs—unless your favorite came on? Do you know the weather, the news, the gossip by the DJs?

Likely not. I know that even though I have had training in active listening, I still fall into bad habits that have come from misconceptions about listening being automatic and easy.

For example, I have one of those weather radios that, at the push of the button, indicates the weather for the day and the week; sometimes it gives unwanted additional information, like the river stages, the coastal predictions, and the major city forecasts for travelers. All I want to know is the day's weather here in my city. But what I find happening is that I start thinking about other things while I am waiting for the day's forecast, and before I know it, the recording from the weather bureau is again playing the same line I heard when I turned it on. I sheepishly admit that I have listened to as many as four rounds of a recording to get the day's weather—all because I too sometimes buy into the misconception that listening to something so simple would be easy. If it were easy, I would have heard it the first time around!

Haven't you ever asked someone to repeat something because you didn't listen effectively the first time? But it is particularly embarrassing when you didn't listen effectively the second time and you wish they would repeat it again because you dare not ask for a third repetition.

I have something else that will show you, beyond a doubt, that you think listening is easy. When you are in a speech class, those of you not speaking on a given day tend to think, "Today I don't have to do anything because I'm not speaking. I get to sit back and relax (listen)."

Since the tendency is for people to think of listening as easy, they also falsely assume that there is no need for special training.

The confusion from this assumption arises from thinking that hearing is listening. Let's differentiate the two words.

"I THOUGHT YOU SAID THE PARTY WAS TONIGHT."

Hearing Is a Biological Function, Occurring Automatically

Hearing is a physical function of the ears, which can be medically checked by a hearing test. Hearing means that an individual's outer ear, middle ear, and inner ear mechanisms allow sounds to be transmitted within the normal human ranges. The process begins with sound causing the eardrum to vibrate, without any conscious help from you. In fact, you have no choice in the matter; it is not something you can choose to stop. Hearing is a biological function.

Listening Is a Mental Choice and Requires Conscious Effort

Though hearing is a biological function, listening is not. Listening means that you consciously attempt to understand what you hear, that you attempt to comprehend its meaning.

If I listen to my weather radio, I comprehend what the weather will be the first time the recording plays, and thus I do not need to play it again. If I listen effectively, I get my brain to register a person's name the first time I hear it and do not have to ask to have it repeated a second, or even a third time.

Listening is not a passive activity but rather takes conscious effort and is hard work; it is an intellectual process. To listen well requires practice because listening is a skill, just like any other skill, including that of public speaking.

Unfortunately, we have a problem with listening that we might not have with other skills we learn. For example, if we wanted to learn how to play either a sport or a musical instrument, we would likely opt to take some lessons. The advantage of having an accomplished teacher is that a pro knows the methods that facilitate learning. In addition, a teacher can watch us and tell us if we are developing a bad habit that will hamper our progress.

Such is not the case with the skill of listening. This skill is rarely taught by parents or teachers, and furthermore, because from the time we are small children, we begin to equate biological hearing with the skill of listening, we already embrace misconceptions and develop bad habits from those early childhood years.

As a result, before we can be trained in the skill of listening, we need to evaluate ourselves to discover what habits we have that detract from our listening effectiveness. Ask yourself the following questions to discover which, if any, bad habits you have.

Are You a Boredom-Dismisser?

How many times have you found yourself doodling on a sheet of paper while listening to a lecture or speech? Usually, the reason people doodle is that they consider the material boring and consider an uninteresting speech to be of little value. These are "boredom-dismissers," who believe what someone says is unimportant if it is uninteresting.

I have often asked students if they would rather hear a funny speaker who has no main points or a boring speaker who has an organized speech. The answer is inevitably the humorous speaker.

But then I ask the question within a little different framework. Let's say that you and Dave have different bosses, but both of you were sent by your company to a third company to work on the same special project. Whichever of you does the best job will get the next one too, and this second job will earn one of you a $5,000 bonus.

Each of your bosses has to explain how the company wants the current job performed. Would you rather your boss be the funny boss who has no organization or the boring boss who gives you the information in an organized, logical breakdown?

Suddenly the boring speaker is no longer so boring. Why? Because the **listener** has decided to be interested in the information. Do not make the mistaken assumption that boring information lacks value. Of course, a good speaker's presentation will be both organized and interesting, but if it is not and if we ask for the humorous one at the exclusion of main ideas, we are choosing a speaker who is a weak communicator.

If you realize that at some time in your life, knowledge that you gain will become useful, maybe even valuable, you can make yourself into a more willing and more effective listener. It is the job of the listener to get the speaker's information, no matter what the speaker's failures. Speaking is one skill; listening is another. Be careful not to blame a speaker for the listeners' bad habits.

Are You an Attention-Faker?

I have heard parents tell their children, "Well, if you are not going to pay attention, you can at least **look** like you are paying attention."

And many of us have learned the deceit well. How many times have you pretended to be paying attention to someone who was talking only to have your name called, shocking you back into the reality that you had no idea what had been going on or why your name was called? We have been "attention-fakers."

What we have effectively learned is how to be dishonest. We have learned to pretend something that is not so. We fake attention because we think it is the polite thing to do.

Faking attention is an act that stops communication from taking place. It is intentionally misleading action to make the speaker think he or she is being listened to. It is a well-rehearsed lie. We need to learn to give honest feedback, even if that feedback is negative. Honesty makes communication possible; dishonesty makes communication impossible.

Are You a Daydreamer?

Very likely, what a person does during a boring speech or at the time of faking attention is to daydream. Dreaming is an occurrence at night when we are asleep. Daydreaming is different only because it occurs in the daytime with open eyes when we are supposedly awake. But we are not awake to the world around us when we are "daydreamers."

Years ago at Wayne State University in Detroit, Professor Paul Cameron conducted research on the listening skills of lecture-hall students. At periodic intervals, a gun was fired and the students recorded their thoughts at that moment. The findings indicated that most students are reminiscing the past, daydreaming the future, or pursuing erotic thoughts. Only 12 percent were found to be active listeners.[2]

It is important for you to check your own habits. Do you tend to daydream when you listen to others talk? Begin to analyze whether you daydream or listen. Check yourself periodically through the day. Try to tune in to what your tendencies are. You cannot change a bad habit until first you know you have one. You cannot modify behavior until you analyze what behavior needs changing.

Even good listeners can sometimes find themselves falling into a daydream, and there is a logical explanation. A human brain has the capacity to listen to speech at a rate close to 600 words per minute, but a speaker usually speaks at a rate between 120 and 140 words per minute. So a listener's brain can comprehend words at a rate between four and five times as fast as a speaker can utter those words. Thus there is a "time lapse" when the listener's brain has no external words to stimulate it and hold its interest. The question becomes, What is the listener going to do with the spare time? The answer, too often, is daydream.

If you can begin to catch yourself when you daydream, you can begin developing good listening practices. Consciously listen to what the speaker says and then repeat the idea in your mind with the extra time you have. Repetition helps sink the idea into your memory bank so you can recall the information when you need it. If you daydream, there will be no information to recall.

Are You a Fact-Finder?

On first evaluation, it may seem positive to find facts in a speech. At least there is indication that the listener was listening. It is true that remembering facts may be good; the negative part of this occurs when the "fact-finder" becomes so intrigued by a set of facts that he or she does not remember the main ideas.

Let's look at what we have learned about the purpose of a speech: The purpose of a speech is to get the audience to remember the main ideas about a topic. The word *main* here is of importance; its definition is "principal," "chief," "most important," or "first in any respect." The reason you speak is you want to communicate an idea to someone else. You choose a topic after analyzing the audience, and then you decide what two, three, or four major ideas about the topic will be worthy information for your audience to remember. These main ideas are put into a thesis statement. It is the thesis that is the deciding factor in what specific details are used. The function of these details is to aid the audience in remembering the main idea by adding interesting anecdotes, case studies, or personal stories. These specifics have no purpose by themselves; they exist solely to prove and to amplify the main idea in order to help the audience remember that "main" idea.

If a listener becomes so intrigued by a specific that he or she remembers the specific at the exclusion of the main idea, then the listener has failed the task of effective listening. The listeners' job is to remember main ideas first; then if some details are also remembered, it is a bonus, an extra.

Are You an Adrenaline-Reactor?

As we saw in Chapter 1, adrenaline charges us up and gives us extra energy. Adrenaline can be secreted by the body in response to excess emotion. Sudden emotion occurs in a variety of situations. Fear is not the only emotion stimulating the body, and hence the speaker in a communication situation may not be the only one who has excess adrenaline. The listener may respond to a speaker nonverbally, and the emotional response can be quite strong.

For example, try this exercise. Think of someone you do not like—perhaps someone you do not get along with at all. Now pretend that you are sitting in a room with many others awaiting a speaker yet to be announced. When the announcement is made, you hear the name of this person you do not like. When that person enters and walks to the front of the room, how are you going to feel? Your emotions will be strongly negative; as a result, your ability to listen effectively is greatly hampered, if not nonexistent. You are now an "adrenaline-reactor"—a listener who lets emotions interfere with your job of listening well. Even if, by chance, the speaker has some very sound ideas, you will not be listening. You are too caught up in your "gut reaction" to be objective.

Likewise, there are certain topics that will automatically increase emotions of some listeners. When they hear one of those volatile topics, they automatically think of their own beliefs about the issue and why those beliefs are right. The problem is that if a person of differing beliefs doesn't stop to listen to the other side, how can he or she know which arguments to refute? We do not have to agree with a speaker to be courteous enough to listen to different ideas.

Are You a Delivery-Emphasizer?

A "delivery-emphasizer" concentrates on some aspect of a speaker's delivery to the exclusion of effectively listening to what is being said.

Many of us fall into this bad habit. If the speaker says "uh" frequently, we begin to predict when the word will come again. I remember what a poor listener I was in one of my high school classes. The teacher was one of those with a pet phrase he repeated over and over and over. So we students placed bets on how many times it would be said in a given class period. By listening only for the repetition, I heard none of the material for the class. I learned nothing, and it took its toll on my next test grade, which proved to be an effective tool to teach me that listening to what is said is far more important than how the message is delivered.

Some listeners notice a speaker's clothing or hair and then turn off to the message if they do not approve. I used to show my students how quickly they could fall into this bad habit by entering the classroom with a section of my hairs sticking straight up from my head. I acted like I did not know about the hair problem and began talking, all the while watching several students smiling and looking at one another and whispering. I could tell some were debating whether to call my attention to it. But the incident always pointed out how easy it is to get caught up in some aspect of the speaker and ignore the speech. The job of the listener is to listen actively to what is being said, not how it is said or how the speaker looks when saying it.

The snares enticing you to become a weak listener are ever present. Any isolated problem can become a bad habit and hamper your listening ability until you put forth the effort to rid yourself of it. The first letters of the six poor listeners previously named spell "Bad Fad":

1. Boredom-Dismisser
2. Attention-Faker
3. Daydreamer
4. Fact-Finder
5. Adrenaline-Reactor
6. Delivery-Emphasizer

By remembering them and their traits, you can analyze your own habits and work on becoming a good listener.

Communication is a two-way process, and even if the speaker does not fulfill his or her obligations, the listener can still fulfill the obligations of effective listening. But there are other ways communication can be hampered, for the communication process involves more than merely a speaker and a listener.

Understand the Communication Cycle

Though you do not have to know the technicalities of a communication cycle in order to speak or listen effectively, knowing a little about the cycle can help prevent potential problems with communication. It is easy to assume that there is a straight-line approach in communication as indicated by the following.

Speaker ——————————————————————— Listener

Note how there are only two factors present: speaker and listener.

Unfortunately, communication is not so simple. There is not a straight line moving from speaker to listener but rather a cycle with many possible interferences to break the circuit. Let's begin again with the speaker, but now let's look at a slightly more comprehensive breakdown of the process, as shown in Figure 14.2.

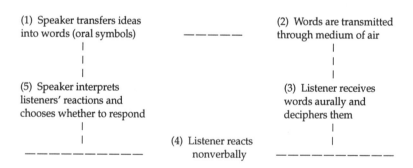

(1) Speaker transfers ideas into words (oral symbols) — — — — — (2) Words are transmitted through medium of air

(5) Speaker interprets listeners' reactions and chooses whether to respond (3) Listener receives words aurally and deciphers them

(4) Listener reacts nonverbally

Figure 14.2. Communication Cycle

Looking at communication in terms of a circle helps us realize that an unbroken circuit means good communication; yet the circuit can break at any of five places, stopping communication. Let's look at each of the potential breaks.

1. The first step in the cycle is that a speaker has an idea and, in order to transmit that thought, he or she encodes the idea into words. A breakdown occurs if the speaker chooses the wrong word. Maybe the speaker has an incorrect definition for a word; maybe he or she merely says the wrong word while thinking the right one was said; maybe a term is used that is too technical for the audience.

Whatever the reason, a wrong word means wrong communication. The simpler the words, the more likely correct communication will result. Beginning speakers often incorrectly assume big words will impress an audience. To the contrary, they usually lose those listeners who do not know the meaning. The simpler the wording, the more likely the communication will succeed.

2. It seems a minor point that words have to travel through the air to get to the listener. But the point becomes major when interference exists. For example, when I decided to get through college in a hurry, I attended summer school. One of my classes was held in an ancient building with no air conditioning. The windows had to be raised to circulate the stale, humid air. For some reason, the administration decided to use this time to replace the sidewalks directly outside the classroom. While a jackhammer roared through the open windows, we in the oven-like classroom tried to listen to a lecturer talking without a microphone. We missed lots of words, and the lecturer became hoarse each day from yelling. The transmitting medium of air is very important.

Another example of the surroundings being important is so simple as an open door. During lectures the audience in line with the open door will encounter temptations to stop listening. For example, haven't you ever noticed that when approaching footsteps are heard down a hallway, the row of listeners in line with the door all turn to see who is walking by? It is human nature to want to turn to follow the noise, and I have been guilty of yielding to the temptation and becoming a poor listener. The surrounding environment can have lots of other distractions: movements by others, extraneous noises, ineffective lighting, inefficient heating or cooling. Be aware of the significance of the transmitting medium and the environment in communication situations; communication can be helped or hampered.

3. As we already know, a breakdown in communication can occur if the listener is ineffective. But there are other barriers that are beyond the listener's immediate control. For example, if the listener does not know the meaning of a word, then the communication intended by the speaker does not occur. If technical terms that are unfamiliar to the listener are being used, the listener cannot suddenly know the meanings. The fault may lie with either the speaker, who may be using inappropriate terminology, or with the listener, who may not have an adequate vocabulary. The important point is that you realize that this place in the communication cycle is a place where communication can break down. Furthermore, remember we already learned that research shows us that a listener *who is working hard to understand and remember* retains only 25 percent of the information.[3] Verbal interaction is a fragile affair.

4. Suppose that the first three places in the cycle remain unbroken. So far, the speaker used appropriate words, there was no interference in the transmitting medium, and the listener deciphers the word meanings correctly. This next breakdown involves the listeners' reactions during a speech—or *audience feedback*. This term means that the audience is always feeding back some kind of reaction to the speaker. Whenever the listener reacts in a way not representing how he or she feels, then incorrect feedback results.

For example, suppose that a listener understands what has been said, but suddenly gets a hunger pain and frowns. At this time, the speaker happens to be looking at this particular listener and interprets that the listener does not understand the information just given. So the speaker reiterates the point in a little different wording. However, in this case, the feedback was inappropriate; in fact, it was not a reaction to anything that was said. So this breakdown occurs when the nonverbal signals a listener sends back to the speaker do not accurately represent the listener's comprehension.

5. The last possible breakdown can occur when the speaker ignores or misinterprets the listeners' feedback, even though the feedback is obvious and accurately reflects the listeners' understanding.

For example, suppose several members of the audience are frowning and giving facial indication that they do not comprehend what the speaker means. If the speaker chooses to ignore the listeners and forges ahead, the speaker has lost a chance to regain these listeners and, as a result, stops the communication circle from being completed.

Likewise, since frowns can be interpreted various ways, suppose the speaker decides that they mean the audience disagrees with what was said. So the speaker, in misinterpreting the feedback, begins defending what he or she said and indicates research that supports that particular position. Communication is harmed because what the audience needed, but didn't get, was further explanation and simplification of the information.

Communication is fragile; it is vulnerable at so many points and in so many ways that it is a wonder we have the successes we do. Perhaps success is easier to achieve when we know where the dangers lurk. By knowing the six barriers to effective listening and the five possible points of breakdown in the communication cycle, we can be on guard against severing communication in either our personal or public relationships.

Build on Your Skills for the Future

Speaking ability is a skill that you will need time and again as you travel through your life. You need it every time you give directions on how to get somewhere, whenever you explain how to perform a certain task, whenever you explain how or why something works or doesn't work; you need speaking skill when you interview for a job, when you request a raise, when you vie for an available promotion. Speaking skill is needed throughout each day, some days less than others, and some days more. The more you make yourself consciously aware of using the techniques in this book, the more likely you are to improve in your ability. The purpose of this book is not to fulfill only a one-semester or one-quarter course requirement. This book's goal is to make you aware that a skill is made better through a lifetime of hard work and continuous practice.

Notes

1. Andrew D. Wolvin and Carolyn Gwynn Coakley, "A Survey of the Status of Listening Training in Some *Fortune* 500 Corporations," *Communication Education*, April 1991, p. 163.

2. Lilly Walters, *Persuasive Platform Presentations*, Walters Speakers Services, Glendora, CA, p. 28. (Used with permission from Walters Speakers Services.)

3. Ralph G. Nichols, "Do We Know How to Listen? Practical Help in a Modern Age," *Speech Teacher*, October 1961, p. 120.

Appendix A

Sample Speech Evaluation Form

NAME _____

TIME OF CLASS_____   SPEAKER #_____

INITIAL SCORE   _____

SPEECH TIME   _____

TOPIC CHOICE +5/0/–5   _____

FINAL SCORE   _____

SPEECH EVALUATION FORM

	EXCELLENT 10 PTS	GOOD 8 PTS	AVG 7 PTS	WEAK 6 PTS
DELIVERY:				
Voice	_____	_____	_____	_____
Grammar/Enunciation	_____	_____	_____	_____
Pauses/Rate	_____	_____	_____	_____
Eye Contact	_____	_____	_____	_____
Gestures/Movement	_____	_____	_____	_____
CONTENT:				
Attention-Getter				
Relevance to Audience	_____	_____	_____	_____
Thesis/Organization Clarity	_____	_____	_____	_____
Body's Organization				
Support/Logic	_____	_____	_____	_____
Transitions	_____	_____	_____	_____
Conclusions	_____	_____	_____	_____

Appendix B

Steps to Follow in Preparing an Information Speech

Now that you have all the steps necessary to prepare a speech, they are listed below in a simplified fashion. If you check each one off as it is completed, you will easily be able to picture what you have done and what you have left to do. If you have a deadline for the speech, you can place how many days you have to do each step beside the respective number.

Steps to Follow in Preparing an Information Speech

1. ANALYZE AUDIENCE

2. CHOOSE TOPIC

3. RESEARCH TOPIC

4. ORGANIZE THESIS

5. SUPPORT THESIS

6. USE TRANSITIONS

7. CREATE INTRODUCTION

8. CREATE CONCLUSION

9. READ ALOUD AND TIME; REVISE AND PLACE ON NOTE CARDS

10. REHEARSE FROM NOTE CARDS, TIME AND REVISE, REHEARSE, REHEARSE, REHEARSE, REHEARSE, REHEARSE, REHEARSE

Appendix C

Sample Assignment for Icebreaker

An icebreaker speech gives you a chance to stand before your classmates and tell them something about yourself. You are not expected to give a long account of your life, but by introducing yourself, your audience will get to know you, you will get the "feel" of standing and talking in front of an audience, and all members of the class can begin a bonding that will help a speech beginner gain courage and confidence.

When you read the questions at the end of this sheet, decide which ones you will answer and how. Jot your ideas on note cards and rehearse four or five times and time yourself each time. Practice aloud, standing in front of a room at home or in an empty classroom. DO NOT MEMORIZE YOUR SPEECH; DO NOT READ YOUR SPEECH. Merely have main ideas jotted on a couple of note cards in LARGE print that is easy to see.

When your number is called, walk quietly to the front of the room, and when you get there, plant your weight evenly on **both** feet; this helps you avoid swaying or moving one foot back and forth. Stand behind the rostrum or podium and place each hand on either side of the top; if you feel comfortable moving around a little, do so, but be sure your movements do not become nervous and that they have purpose. Talk just a little louder than your normal voice so that every single person in the room can hear you without straining. Look at various individuals directly in the eyes for four or five seconds and look at people in different areas of the audience. Be careful not to favor one person or one group in a small area of the room.

When you are ready to end your remarks, conclude with a brief summarizing statement—not, "Well, I guess that's all." Rather, plan a wrap-up sentence that summarizes the main categories you've discussed, or leave the audience thinking about something you've said, or say something to help everyone remember your name. In other words, think of something meaningful. Pause at least two seconds after your final words; then (even though you may want to collapse or heave a big sigh of relief or run to your chair), go easily and quietly to your seat. Do not rush, or crumple your notes into a wad and stuff them in your pocket. Avoid the nonverbal signals that say, "Whew! Am I glad that's over!" In this case, advertising does not pay; outer control does. Remember that even when you walk to your seat and sit down, people are still watching you and you are still giving an impression of yourself. Make it a positive one.

AREAS TO CONSIDER FOR PREPARATION OF SELF-INTRODUCTION ICEBREAKER SPEECH

I. Facts About Yourself
   A. Name
   B. Area of town you live in
   C. Your major and what company you eventually want to work for
   D. Why you chose this college
   E. Other colleges you have attended
   F. Job you hold and hours you work
   G. Where you want to live after you graduate
II. Hobbies and Interests
   A. Sports you watch or play
   B. Music you listen to or instruments you play
   C. Favorite reading materials
   D. Crafts you do or want to learn
   E. Volunteer work
III. Memorable Experiences
   A. A frightening experience
   B. An embarrassing experience
   C. A sad experience
   D. A particularly rewarding experience (monetarily or emotionally)
IV. Influential People
   A. Family
   B. Friends
   C. Priests/Ministers/Rabbis/Counselors/and so forth

Choose from the list what you think will interest your audience, and then time your speech to around five minutes. In advance of your speech, prepare to hand in an outline on 8½ × 11 paper; therefore, put your notes that you use when you deliver your speech on separate paper or on 4 × 6 note cards, according to your teacher's instructions.

Make your outline follow the same type of arrangement given above. You just need to pick which areas you wish to discuss and then fill in the categories with specifics.

Remember, it is normal and even desirable to have speech fear. If you have it, you are doing something right, not wrong!

Index

About the Author

Rebecca McDaniel earned bachelor's and master's degrees in both speech and English at Ball State University, Muncie, Indiana. She is currently Associate Professor of Speech and English at Raymond Walters College, University of Cincinnati, a position she has held since 1972.

As a teacher of speech, two repeated problems left an impact on her: The fear that often inhibits beginners when they are faced with speaking in front of a group, and beginners' lack of knowledge that speaking is a simple step-by-step process. The recurrence of these problems was the catalyst for two major projects: (1) the writing of *Scared Speechless: Public Speaking Step by Step,* and (2) the start of a part-time business, McDaniel Consulting for Successful Speaking and Writing. The intent of both projects is to help beginners both in and out of school learn how to cope with speech fear and how to understand the step-by-step process necessary to prepare and deliver a speech.

Her publications include an article in *The Cincinnati Enquirer Magazine,* a 1990 English text- and workbook coauthored with Barbara Hansen, *Developing Sentence Skills,* and a coauthored radio program about the use of songs in advertising that aired on the *Dusty Rhodes Show* (700 WLW AM, May 1, 1988).